A Sea Within

The Gulf of St. Lawrence

QUEBEC
Outardes R.
Moisie R.
Mingan R.
Romaine R.
Watshishou R.
Natashquan R.
Olomane R.
Etamamu R.
St. Augustin R.
L'Anse Amour
Blanc Sablon
Old Fort Bay
Bradore B.
Strait of Belle Is.
L'Anse aux Meadows
Cape Bauld
Bonne Esperance B.
Shekatika
La Tabatière
Mutton Bay
Tête-à-la-Baleine
Harrington Harbour
Port aux Choix
Pte. Riche
GREAT NORTHERN PENINSULA
Sept Iles
Mingan Is.
Havre St. Pierre
Baie Johann Baetz
Baie St. Lawrence
Natashquan
Kegaska
Musquaro
Godbout R.
Ellis Bay
Jupiter R.
ANTICOSTI I.
Bonne B.
Trout River
Humber R.
Pte. des Monts
GASPÉ PASSAGE
Fox Bay
Heath Point
Egg Island
Cap Chat
Ste Anne des Monts
Matane
C. Rosiers
Gaspé B.
NEWFOUNDLAND
Saguenay R.
Rimouski
GASPÉ PENINSULA
Percé
Bonaventure I.
Port au Port
Tadoussac
Paspébiac
GULF OF ST. LAWRENCE
Restigouche
Chaleur Bay
Miscou I.
Shippegan I.
Bird Rocks
Ile Brion
Cape Anguille
Magdalen Islands
Port aux Basques
NEW BRUNSWICK
Miramichi B.
CABOT STRAIT
N
Tignish
Cape North
Miquelon
St. Pierre
Richibucto
Malpeque B.
Cheticamp
CAPE BRETON I.
Margaree Harbour
P.E.I.
Charlottetown
Hillsborough R.
Shediac
Inverness
Cape Tormentine
Prim Pt.
Chignecto Peninsula
Ft. Beauséjour
Ft. Lawrence
Pictou
BAY OF FUNDY
NOVA SCOTIA

A Sea Within
The Gulf of St. Lawrence

Bruce Litteljohn and Wayland Drew

McClelland and Stewart

The Canadian Publishers
McClelland and Stewart Limited
25 Hollinger Road
Toronto, M4B 3G2

CANADIAN CATALOGUING IN PUBLICATION DATA

Litteljohn, Bruce M., 1935-
A sea within : the Gulf of St. Lawrence

ISBN 0-7710-5318-5

1. St. Lawrence, Gulf of – Description and travel.
I. Drew, Wayland, 1932- II. Title.

FC2004.L57 1984 917.1'096344 C84-098220-8
F1050.L57 1984

PAGES SIX AND SEVEN: BOAT LEAVING GRANDE ENTRÉE, MAGDALEN ISLANDS, QUEBEC

Design by Tad Aronowicz

Printed and bound in Hong Kong by Scanner Art Services Inc. Toronto

For Marda and James McNab, and Christopher, Sean, and Meghan Litteljohn

The Gulf of St. Lawrence grows across the old maps like a starfish, stretching west. It holds fast to the Atlantic through the Strait of Belle Isle and the Cabot Strait; it encircles Prince Edward Island with two other arms; and with the fifth it reaches far into the heart of the continent. This western arm, the longest, points past what is known – Anticosti Island, the shoulder of the Gaspé Peninsula, and the rich estuaries of the north shore – points towards a mystery. The tip of it rests at *kebec*, the narrows.

At Quebec the Gulf of St. Lawrence begins and ends. Geographers will draw other lines to separate the river from the estuary, and the estuary from the Gulf, but the land makes its own distinctions – the land and the sea. Salt air drifts across Ile d'Orléans, and Quebec feels the pulse of the tides.

Through the centuries, mariners arriving in Canada have been subtly enfolded by the land until they reached this narrows. Enticed by mystery, enticed by wealth, many passed through, adopted the light boats of the inhabitants, and kept moving west. Others were drawn back to the sea again, their vessels carried by currents and westerlies down the broadening estuary, across the inland sea that is the Gulf, and out through one of its straits towards Bristol, or Brittany, or Spain. For all, Quebec was either the beginning of a journey or an end. And so it is to this day.

Nothing in time and space corresponds to the neat configuration labelled "Gulf of St. Lawrence" on geographers' maps. A gulf by definition is an emptiness. In gulfs time stops, and no relationship survives. Shelley referred to death itself as a gulf. Tennyson's Ulysses foresaw himself and his men washed down in unknown gulfs, and St. Luke has Abraham say with eternal sadness to the rich man, "Between us and you there is a great gulf fixed."

But the mind cannot maintain the notion of a vacuum. Images rush to fill it. Journey into the centre of the Gulf of St. Lawrence and you will find not emptiness but soft kaleidoscopes of spindrift and phosphorescence; not an end, but myriad beginnings. Coast in the wakes of the discoverers and you will find no gulf but a splendid profusion of life, an endless procession of sight and sound: a raven hovering above the Bradore bluffs; the awesome presence of a passing iceberg; the blowing of a pod of humpbacks; the incomparable beaches of the Magdalens; little boats setting out in the face of advancing storms; the ghostly notes of foghorns drifting through the cemeteries of Newfoundland; the sea, and the vestiges of generations who have lived out their lives beside it.

It is such things that are celebrated here in word and photograph. The real Gulf lies in the interstices among them.

Today at Pointe des Monts the land remains as it was three centuries ago. Gulls ride updrafts above the mingling of sea and rock. Tidewater spreads in smooth sheets across the granite. A foghorn growls at

LEFT: TRACADIE, PRINCE EDWARD ISLAND

RIGHT: LOURDES DE BLANC SABLON, QUEBEC

thirty-second intervals and a brisk light flashes atop a skeletal frame. The fathom-thick walls of the old and darkened lighthouse, mortared in 1830, taper cleanly up to the light deck.

If you voyage from Quebec to this place, sensing the river broaden infinitesimally until at last the south shore drifts behind fog mirages that conjure mountains where there are no mountains, islands where the chart shows a blue void, you would not need to watch your pilot disembark to know that you had at last reached the sea. Its iodine will fill your nostrils, and its rhythms will long since have crept up through the decking beneath your feet. It lies ahead, to the east; a horizon. Grey on lighter grey if the day is clear, it is swathed in fogs if warm air moves across it.

The geographers' Gulf of St. Lawrence is a measurable entity, stretching 670 kilometres from the old lighthouse at Pointe des Monts to Bonne Bay on the western shore of Newfoundland, and 515 kilometres from Johann Baetz's lonely manor house on the north shore to the bubbling coal gases of Pictou on the south. Cradled in the arm of the south shore is Prince Edward Island. At the centre is the scimitar of the Magdalen archipelago. Thrust like a thumb into the throat of the river is Anticosti Island. If you drop a weighted line into the Laurentian Channel north of the Magdalens, it will sink almost 500 metres before it touches bottom. It is the warmer of Canada's two great inland seas, this Gulf, and smaller than Hudson Bay. Breton fishermen called it La Grande Baie; we do not know what name the native peoples gave it or, indeed, whether they conceived of it as a thing separate from its various coasts and islands.

Its contrasts are striking. Around its southern coast and in the sandy shallows of Prince Edward Island, the summer sea is almost tropically warm; but north, through the Strait of Belle Isle, the Labrador Current brushes the north shore and swirls down into the Gulf, bearing beluga whales and icebergs. The landforms, too, vary widely. The north end of the Appalachian chain reaches up through Gaspé's Chic Chocs and ends in the Long Range Mountains of Newfoundland, and the renowned hills of Cape Breton brood over the Cabot Trail; but throughout the Gulf slender promontories reach into the sea like the wrinkled fingers of old men, and in some lights the wispy beaches of Prince Edward Island and the Magdalens lie like mere threads on the horizon. Some areas, like Chaleur Bay, are welcoming; some, like Belle Isle, are forbidding. Human effects, too, are more apparent in some regions than in others. Several cities lie on the Gulf coasts, and in the southern arms there are few shores not lit at night by the lamps of dwellings and lighthouses; but north, towards Labrador, the stone land slumbers as it has forever, with only tiny settlements clinging to its flanks.

It is inestimably old, that land, the oldest on earth. Against it, the whole of the human drama is insignificant. In *Basin and Range*, John McPhee suggests the best way to conceive its age: "With your arms spread wide ... to represent all time on earth, look at one hand with its line of life. The Cambrian begins in the wrist, and the Permian extinction is at the outer end of the palm. All of the Cenozoic is in a fingerprint, and in a single stroke with a medium-grained nail file you could eradicate human history."

For a time following their formation 900 million years ago the bedrocks of the Gulf were split and folded, overlaid with breccia and gravel-like conglomerate spewed from countless volcanoes as the rims of shifting continental plates ground together. This tectonic mayhem lasted 375 million years and produced the Appalachians. In their prime these mountains rivalled the Rockies and even now, eroded, in certain lights at certain places they are awesome still. A vast weight of time has passed across them.

Late in the Paleozoic Era they were washed by the sea itself. During or after this submergence, the whole Precambrian table and its billions of tons of shale and limestone overburden were broken by more eruptions. Upheaved chunks settled at crazy angles; the entire island of Newfoundland tilts down from west to east. Millennia of more folding, more faulting, more volcanoes, and still more erosion followed. Finally, about one million years ago, the region was glaciated at least once and probably twice. A grinding maul of ice several thousand feet thick was the last great shaper of the Gulf. It sheared off escarpments and gouged valleys for the Gulf's 200 rivers. It left granite hilltops curved like the cowls of monks. It shifted boulders from Labrador and Ungava onto Gulf headlands and left them like counters in some inscrutable game abandoned by the gods. Its weight compressed the landmass like a gigantic sponge, so that ever since its melting 10,000 years ago the land has been rising back up out of itself, bearing with it the strands of ancient beaches and the remnants of primordial tides.

Creation continues. Ice, wind, and rain fracture and erode the bedrock as surely as burgeoning and decaying forests change the contours of the soil, as surely as the incessant sea sculpts the shores. But in the vistas of eons, 10,000 years is but a little interval. In that time the Gulf has changed only slightly. It is much the same today as it was when the first men, pursuing their game eastward along the melting edges of the ice, came to its shores.

*I*n some places it is especially easy to re-enter that ancient time.

On the western shore of Newfoundland's Great Northern Peninsula lies a region with the evocative name of Gros Morne. It is one of the most diverse and fascinating areas of the coast. Bonne Bay stretches along its southern edge, a deep indentation wide enough to harbour whales. Several hamlets touch the bay with docks, warehouses, and boatyards: Rocky Harbour, Norris Point, Shoal Brook, and Lomond. One village, Woody Point, boasts a jaunty line of Lombardy poplars between its main road and the shore, planted by someone who took the Newfoundland craving for domesticity to an Italianate extreme. To the traveller entering Woody Point after a journey up the harsh coast, these poplars with their sentinels' dressing are at first strangely incongruous. That they are really appropriate the traveller

ABOVE: NET MENDING, SEPT ILES, QUEBEC

OPPOSITE: ESCUMINAC FLATS, CHALEUR BAY, QUEBEC

will realize if he lingers awhile, for the atmosphere of Bonne Bay is actually domestic and cultivated. Indeed, with its steep green hillsides and quiet coves it seems like a secluded corner of China. A little ferryboat rocks gently in its passages across the bay. Browsing humpbacks roam along the shore.

Yet, behind the decorous oriental hills loom sombre and troubling presences. New arrivals pass one of these and cannot help seeing it, although few stop for photographs. Crossing Bonne Bay one sees it rising squarely above its ring of tranquil knolls. It is the Tableland, 100 kilometres square and over 600 metres high, a remnant of the earth's magma, older even than the Precambrian bedrock, as old as the first cooling of this spinning sphere of gas and liquid. Its top is flat, sheared off by ancient rivers. It dominates the region and commands.

Not every visitor will answer its summons. Those who do will follow the road from Bonne Bay towards Trout River and, after two or three kilometres, enter an arid canyon. To the east the Tableland rises sharply, fans of snow draped in its crevices even late into the summer. To the west, lower hills slope to the sea. The vegetation is sparse and stunted – grasses, lichens, pitcher-plants, a few mosses near a stream bed. Capricious gusts curve from the sea and bounce at random off the hills. Ravens drift above the summits.

At 300 metres there is profound emptiness. The last scraggly bits of herbage vanish. The few gulls whose soft mewing, like the admonitions of fretting ghosts, have accompanied the climber this far, wheel away and drop into the valleys. The rock gleams with ceramic veneer – the mineral serpentine, transformed by ancient suns and vaporizing chemicals, pale green, faceted sometimes like elegant cloisonné, scaled sometimes like heavy lizard skin. The boulders grow bigger, as do the fissures among them. Climbing becomes a perilous leaping; one could die here, attended only by insects.

On top is the reward: to stand in a landscape sublimely still and barren and to gaze across the hilltops and out to sea. North beyond seeing lies the Strait of Belle Isle where the promontories at the tip of Newfoundland grip the sea like dark talons. West, across the Strait, stretch the great beaches, headlands, and estuaries of Quebec and Labrador. To the south lie the islands of the Gulf and the hospitable harbours of New Brunswick and Nova Scotia. To the east, on the other side of the peninsula and down the far, chafed coast, the beaches and coves of Newfoundland are as welcoming as ever, and in the peatlands behind them bloom wild rose, cranberry, cloudberry, Labrador tea, blue iris, and various types of orchids. Caribou and moose stalk the windswept uplands and the forests of sheltered valleys.

Cartographers have taught us to think of the Gulf like this, as a surrounding whole. But there have been many other ways of knowing the Gulf as well. One was that of the first shaggy hunter who climbed a crest on the Quebec shore to gaze out at familiar icebergs and familiar water, but at a new sea and an enticing new shore in the distance. All his life he would go where he was led by the quest

NEAR GROSSES ROCHES, GASPE PENINSULA, QUEBEC

for food, and if the sea and the land offered plenty in any place, then he would stay until that plenty was depleted. Security was food for several days together; happiness, a warm shelter and a laughing woman and a child. Beyond, who knew what the shore might yield? Who knew where one would leave one's bones to be picked by ravens? Day by day, journey by journey, proceeding ever deeper into mystery – that was a way of knowing the Gulf, although most of the words which contained that knowledge have been long since forgotten: the words for walrus and caribou, for lobster and cod and eel. The primitive hunter's way of knowing was the first, and the longest.

Later, others came. Viking knowledge bore memories of Greenland glaciers, and longings for the farms at the heads of the fiords, and a love of the stars and the sea-rhythms and the singing of the steering-oar beneath one's arm. To those first Norsemen who probed through the Strait of Belle Isle in their tall-prowed ship, all would have been familiar – the chill of an unseen iceberg in the night; the lowering headlands; the rivermouths and beaches backed by black spruce and tamarack; the profusion of mosses, berries, and grasses; the colonies of seabirds shrieking on the cliffs; the undulant rising of the whales. All would have been familiar, except that this coast was not home and, therefore, consisted of but a series of landmarks for the journey back, landmarks to be recorded in song and litany. This was another way of knowing the Gulf: with the assessing knowledge of the stranger who would be returning home elsewhere, bearing news.

The settler's way was different again. Immigrants came with the surety that there would be no returning, that they would mine and farm and fish on these strange shores, growing intimate only with what lay within a few leagues' radius, threatened by fog lurking beyond, and by the dark figures that moved in it. To endure in that new land, to see children and crops take root, and to know that because you and your comrades were the first therefore everything you accomplished was also first ... that, too, was a special knowledge, stern and proud, both an affirmation and a denial of history.

Over the centuries the shores of the Gulf have seen the arrival and settling of many different Europeans: the first Norsemen at L'Anse aux Meadows; the first Basque whalers to winter over in the Strait of Belle Isle; the first Breton fishermen left behind to tend shore installations until the return of ships in the spring; the first deckhand to desert a British frigate and find a snug hideaway on the west coast of Newfoundland; the first castaways on the Magdalens. All these brought lonely ways of knowing portions of the Gulf, and all preceded official explorations.

Cartier's voyages in 1534 and 1535 confirmed the rumours in European ports: there was to the west an inland sea of uncertain size phenomenally rich in whale and walrus, abundant in birds and fish. Cartier formed the earliest surviving comprehensive view of the Gulf and the middle reaches of the river. He stands at the beginning of the modern era of navigation in the region. After Cartier, Europeans travelling Gulf waters would know approximately what land masses hemmed them in, and at what distances. Theirs was the last of the ways of knowing the Gulf: as an immutable entity.

No modern person can escape that view. We carry flat maps in our heads. We know what lies around us because we have named so many things and places. First we seed and cultivate the words, and later the words claim us, control our ways of seeing and thinking. Is it to escape such constrictions that we seek the lonely places of the world – islands, remote coasts, and old mountains? Perhaps such places are the last temples, the last of the sacred groves where mystery might still be found. In them we acknowledge the inadequacies of names. What words can express the idea of 900 million years, the age of the Tableland? If such words existed, should we use them? Part of nature, apart from nature, we return to such places to sense eternity and to empty ourselves of thought.

Across Gros Morne and the Tableland, horizons contract with drifting fog. Dusk creeps close. The wind grows cold. Memories of maps blur and fade. Long shadows touch a racial memory. The difference between the body in synthetic fabric and the body wrapped in skins becomes no deeper than their coverings.

Pointe Amour lies about 225 kilometres north of Bonne Bay, where the Strait of Belle Isle is narrowest. It is a crooked finger on the north side of Forteau Bay, beckoning to icebergs and ships alike. At the fog-shrouded entrance to the Gulf, it has one of the dreariest records of any place in Canada. Even after the building of the lighthouse in 1885, two British warships were lost on Pointe Amour, HMS *Lily* in 1889 and HMS *Raleigh* in 1922.

Fragments of the *Raleigh* litter the beach beneath the light, and the graves of drowned sailors are marked with a single monument nearby. Farther inshore lies another, more enigmatic, grave. The two cemeteries are separated by less than a kilometre, by 7,000 years, and by a provocative irony.

The *Raleigh* was the latest and best of modern warships. At the time of her foundering, on 9 August 1922, she had been in service for just over a year. One hundred and eighty-five metres long, she had been designed in 1915 to meet the challenge of German cruisers in the Atlantic, and she was fitted with the most up-to-date defences and armaments. She was the flagship of the North Atlantic Squadron.

At the time of her grounding she was going dead slow. Dense fog had lain across the Strait for several days, and the *Raleigh* was groping through it to rendezvous with her tender, *Calcutta*, already at anchor in Forteau Bay. Unobserved by the helmsman, the sinewy and insidious currents of the Strait tugged the ship several degrees off course to starboard.

She could scarcely have struck at a more desolate spot. Cold and fog-shrouded for much of the year, the northern entrance to the Gulf was only sparsely populated, and its people clustered in isolated

FISHERMEN'S STORAGE SHED, NORTHPORT, PRINCE EDWARD ISLAND

L'ANSE AU GRIFFON, GASPÉ PENINSULA, QUEBEC

villages. In summer, except for the occasional footpath or cart-track along the sea, communication was by water only, by oar or sail. Snow made the upland meadows passable, although few outporters travelled in winter except to hunt and gather wood. Throughout the year icebergs passed through the Strait, sometimes drifting into Forteau Bay and grounding there, melting slowly, ominous reminders to all of the winter they had just survived and of the fresh one coming down upon them.

Many ships had come to grief along that shore, and their crews and passengers had perished with only the wind to hear their cries. Surveying the coast in 1828, Captain Edward Boxer of HMS *Hussar* urged the immediate building of lighthouses at strategic points. "It was truly lamentable Sir, [he wrote] the number of wrecks we saw on the different parts of the coast ... for the number of lives lost must be very great, and property incalculable."

The *Raleigh* was more fortunate than earlier wrecks. Her wireless quickly dispatched news of the accident and the messages sped south, relayed through Fogo. Ships of the North Atlantic Squadron stationed in Bermuda hastened north immediately. The *Empress of France*, which had left Quebec for Cherbourg at four forty-five that afternoon, was ordered to proceed to the Strait with all speed to take on survivors and to render whatever other assistance might be required. The destroyers *Patriot* and *Patrician*, lying at Quebec, were placed on two-hour alert to steam north at Admiralty request. The US Navy Department signalled: "The Department deeply regrets and offers any assistance you desire. Division of battleships now at Halifax and seagoing tugs available at Boston and Newport."

The officers of the *Raleigh*, however, saw no immediate cause for alarm. The Pointe Amour lightkeeper signalled that the ship was lying "easily" and was "apparently in no great danger." Most crewmen were landed safely and installed in makeshift tents on the grounds of the light-station and amidst the extensive sand dunes which lie to the west of Pointe Amour. The following morning Admiral Sir William Pakenham declined with thanks the offers from the *Empress of France* and from the Canadian and US navies.

Unfortunately, bow damage was more extensive than had at first appeared, and in the storms of the following days and weeks the warship was mangled beyond any hope of repair. A sad hulk, she was finally stripped of all salvageable parts, lined with explosives, and ignominiously destroyed.

Ten men had died in the flooding of her forward compartments. One by one their bodies were recovered during August and September, and they were buried in a common grave on the hillside overlooking the wreckage of their ship and the vastness of the Gulf to the south.

The other known grave at L'Anse Amour lies a few hundred yards to the north and on a little plateau above the sea, looking out to the brooding blue line of Newfoundland nineteen kilometres away. It is the grave of a child of twelve whose name we do not know, for in the short distance between the sailors' grave and the child's there lies an abyss of time. The child died 7,500 years ago, 2,000 years before the pyramids were built. His grave is the oldest so far discovered in North America.

He was buried face down, his head to the west, a large rock on his back. Around his neck hung a bone pendant, and interred with him were his knives, his spear-points, and his flute. His body and possessions had been liberally sprinkled with red ochre, a substance which had a mystical significance for his people. Small fires had flickered at the sides of his body. We do not know how he died.

He was a member of the oldest known group to have inhabited the shores of the Gulf: the Boreal (or Maritime) Archaic Indian. Generations of the boy's ancestors may have journeyed north from Nova Scotia as the last ice-sheet receded; or possibly they came from the northwest across the ice-cap itself, pursuing the shifting herds of caribou. Their stone tools have been found across the north – at Old Crow in the Yukon, near Lake Superior, at Seghundhia on Manitoulin Island, and here on the Gulf.

Below the grave, an ice-cold rivulet drains off the plateau and meanders to the sea. Amidst the dunes surrounding the mouth of this stream the boy and his ancestors lived during the warm months of the year. In winter, when snow covered the spongy inland brush and the muskeg, they would follow the caribou; but by the time the harp seals began to whelp on the pack ice of the Gulf they would return to L'Anse Amour and raise skin homes in the shelter of the dunes. They would stay through the summer and the fall. Great auks lived there then, and walrus, and plentiful whales. Occasionally a famished polar bear would abandon an iceberg in Forteau Bay and fall prey to the lances of the circling boats.

For at least 10,000 years people lived among the dunes of L'Anse Amour, and the dunes, shifting still, cover and reveal the detritus of their passage: the points of arrows, lances, and harpoons; gouges and adzes; knives and scrapers; awls and punches; the counters of games; tiny, enigmatic crescent stones.

If you hold one of these tools of that ancient people, if you stand where they once lived and you look down the shore of Pointe Amour to the mangled remains of the *Raleigh*, you will be bemused by the conjunction of symbols. For 10,000 years people lived on the shores of the Gulf and left it still abundant with life. Within only 300 years, Europeans depleted and, in some cases, exhausted that abundance.

If the story of human habitation around the Gulf begins at L'Anse Amour, it begins with these symbols: a stone tool, adequate for survival, inadequate for the domination of nature; a broken warship, instrument of domination, useless for survival in nature. One of them was sufficient for 10,000 years. One of them represents a sane and successful society.

Eventually, the Archaic Indians crossed the Strait of Belle Isle, landed in Newfoundland, and made their way down both coasts of the island. Their distinctive implements have been found at Bonavista Bay on

CHETICAMP, CAPE BRETON ISLAND, NOVA SCOTIA

L'ANSE AU DIABLE, STRAIT OF BELLE ISLE, LABRADOR, NEWFOUNDLAND

the Atlantic side and at Port aux Choix on the Gulf side. Of the two Newfoundland sites, Port aux Choix is the more interesting because a large, ceremonial cemetery has been uncovered there, and because, at this location, the transition of stewardship of Gulf resources from the Archaic people to their successors, the Dorsets, can be traced more clearly.

The harbour at Port aux Choix provides one of the best shelters on the west coast of the island. The name probably comes from the Basque, *portuichoa*, "little harbour." It lies secluded behind the back arm of the Pointe Riche Peninsula. To the south is the sweep of Ingornachoix Bay; to the north lies St. John Island where, long after the passing of the original inhabitants, French, English, and Yankee corsairs would lie in wait for rich cargoes passing through the Strait. To the west of Port aux Choix the whaleback peninsula slopes down to Pointe Riche and the sea.

The ancient cemetery lies at the centre of the village, in a large and sandy bowl. Ninety skeletons have been discovered there, some straight, some flexed in a fetal position for return to the womb of earth, all anointed with the same red ochre that had been sprinkled on the dead youth at L'Anse Amour. Buried with them were tools, sewing implements, weapons, adornments, and personal items, including elegantly smooth slate bayonets and slender bone combs that rival in grace those of Minoan Crete. There were also various magical objects such as stone amulets, the teeth of dogs and bears, and the feet and bills of loons and other seabirds. Neither here nor at L'Anse Amour has any evidence of pottery been found.

In one grave, a child was buried in the embrace of its mother.

These people, their ancestors and descendants, lived on the shores of the Gulf for 10,000 years. They made objects of great beauty, and their respect and love for one another continued into death. How much more is needed to call a people civilized?

About 3,000 years ago, a new people reached the Strait of Belle Isle and spread southward into the Gulf. These were the Dorset Eskimos. Larger than other Inuit, they were people of the sea and lived on the coasts both winter and summer. The excavations over which they erected their skin tents have been found along the Labrador coast and as far west as Anticosti. They have also been found down both coasts of the Great Northern Peninsula.

The depressions at Port aux Choix, on the raised beaches around Pointe Riche, are typical – so shallow that they are almost obscured by the blowing beach grasses, wildflowers, and tuckamore. They are littered with the usual detritus of prehistoric life: stone chips and cores, implements, toys and amulets. Dorset artifacts tend to be very small, and their amulets (frequently depicting bears) are exquisitely finished.

There are many house sites at Port aux Choix, for the Dorsets populated the Gulf for about 1,500 years. Each house was roughly five metres square, with a central hearth and a raised sleeping platform opposite the entrance. Cobble walls and rafters of bone or wood supported a dome of sewn hides. Also at Port aux Choix is an enormous ossuary of seal bones covering several hectares, for Pointe Riche was a favoured sealing spot. Here in the spring the pack ice with its burden of thousands of whelping seals would be blown against the shore, and the hunters could venture safely out.

No record remains of the period of transition during which the Dorsets gained control of the region from their Archaic predecessors. Like encounters between other cultures for the essential resources of life, it was no doubt violent. But there must have been peaces, too; truces, intervals of calm and accommodation, perhaps even periods of co-operation. The Dorsets seem to have learned from the Archaic Indians the use of the toggling harpoon, designed with a detachable head which would twist off and hold in the wound of a plunging sea mammal; and from the Dorsets the Indians might have gained the bow and arrow.

By the time the first Norse longships swept through the Strait of Belle Isle, the Dorsets dominated the Gulf. They therefore had the dubious honour of welcoming the pallid newcomers. Of course we do not know what they thought, or what overtures they made. Probably they were no more enthusiastic about this violation of their space than the Indians had been about the Dorsets' arrival. To the Norse, the Dorsets were simply *skraelings*, "wretches"; noxious and inferior savages to be eliminated as swiftly as possible. The Vikings landed with axes swinging, and their first known casualties were eight Dorsets surprised sleeping beneath their boats. For the race as a whole the coming of the whites was an ominous augury; shortly afterward they vanished from the region. Perhaps changing climatic conditions had altered the movement of sea mammals in the Gulf, forcing them to migrate once again. We do not know what finally became of them.

As for the people they had replaced, the Maritime Archaic Indians, some archaeologists believe that they declined to extinction, while others suspect that they blended in time with the Algonquins and the Hurons. Still others think that they retreated to the interior or to the remoter coasts, and that the hapless Beothuks, later hunted down for sport in Newfoundland, were their descendants. There are haunting similarities, most notably the Beothuks' fondness for the red ochre of the ancient people, a fondness which earned them the epithet *red Indians*.

By the early 1500s, when Europeans began to settle in the Gulf in significant numbers, the aboriginal inhabitants were dispersed roughly into the following groups. In Newfoundland were the Beothuks. Peaceful and secretive, skilled engravers of bone and ivory, they would be slaughtered within

ABOVE: BRADORE BAY, QUEBEC

OPPOSITE: LOURDES DE BLANC SABLON, QUEBEC

two centuries and their crafts and history destroyed. North of the Strait of Belle Isle, and probing occasionally into the Gulf, were the Thule-Labrador Eskimos. Southward from the Strait, ranging across the Labrador tundra in the winter and returning to ancestral sea resorts for the summer, were the Montagnais-Naskapi. Around the south shores, through Gaspé and down the coast of New Brunswick ranged the Micmacs, some of whose territory was shared with the Malecites and Abnakis from the south. From the west, Huron-Iroquois also resorted to the sea in summer.

Boundaries were fluctuating and uncertain, determined more by the vagaries of prey than by any firm notion of possession; but throughout the Gulf Precolumbian peoples lived, travelled, quarrelled, celebrated, worshipped, and died for several thousand years. They were resourceful and tough. In their various languages they would have had the equivalent of the Greek noun *oikos*, "house," although they would have been bewildered by its later splitting into *economics* and *ecology*. For them there was no difference; what was good for the land and the sea was also good for them, for they were creatures of both.

"In all truth," wrote the Basque novelist Pío Baroja, "the sea annihilates a man ... draws him into complaisance ... All of us, without knowing why, assume that the sea is a woman."

Máre, mer, mère. In the saline womb of the sea we were first nourished; the shock of birth is the shock of drying. Ultramarine satisfies our medulla. When we sleep, or lie wrapped in illness, it is the pulse of the sea that we hear against our pillows. Our longing to know the great mammals of the sea arises from our sense that they are more fortunate, perhaps wiser, for they went back to the sea again.

All roads lead to the sea and into the sea, for there are paths in water more ancient than the oldest on the land.

In the North Atlantic, spring is the favoured time for western voyages, because then the Icelandic low-pressure system, static through the winter, shifts northwest and draws the winds behind. For a short time the prevailing westerlies become the easterlies on which the first European adventurers came to North America. Borne on these winds, vessels from the fiords of Greenland will make a landfall on the south coast of Labrador, or near the tip of Newfoundland's northern peninsula.

The names of the bays, landmarks, and villages in that region testify to long familiarity with Breton caravels: Croque, Pointe Enragée, Fishot, Bréhat, St. Lunaire, Griquet, Quirpon (or Karpon, from the Breton *ker*, home or village), Ha Ha Bay (a cul-de-sac, named after a military trap), Trompe l'Oeil Point. Many place-names date from the sixteenth century, but they are relatively recent compared to earlier ones that have been forgotten. The French name for L'Anse aux Meadows has prevailed (a corruption of "L'Anse aux Meduses," bay of jellyfish), but we do not know the Norse name for the place, and it is with the Norse that the bay has become associated.

Near L'Anse aux Meadows is an enigmatic hint that other mariners preceded even the Norse. Celtic legend venerates the memory of St. Brendan, who abandoned the bureaucratic task of managing the abbey at Clonfert, enticed away by the murmur of the sea and the easterlies of spring. Legend says that two other restive anchorites, Barrind and Mernoc, had gone before and had brought back tales of a place so rich that they called it the promised land of the saints. Legend says further that Brendan yielded to the pull of the sea, and went, and that his book, the *Navigatio,* is a record of that journey, however elliptical and fancifully embellished it may be.

Celtic wanderlust was extraordinary. "Where is the wave that can set my people free?" asked the Breton poet Jean Pierre Callog'h. "Where is the lonely isle where do not languish the dead of the Celts?"

While the Archaic Indians and the Dorset Eskimos were spreading along the shores of the Gulf, the Celts, rising from Indo-European stock about 4,000 years ago, and driven by droughts, were pushing westward across the Balkan Peninsula and into Europe. By 800 BC they had established a culture which reached across Europe to Gaul (soon to become the Celtic heartland), down into northern Spain, and up into Britain, Scotland, and Ireland. Caesar respected the Celts as formidable enemies, both on land and sea. He said they were accomplished navigators and had ships capable of lengthy voyages. In time, his legions battled them first in northern Italy, then in Spain and Gaul, and eventually across the Channel in Britain. The remote coasts of Ireland and Scotland north of Hadrian's Wall became the last Celtic strongholds. These never fell to Roman military might, but were penetrated finally by missionaries working north in the wake of the legions. Once Christianized, these northern Celts sent their own monks in a kind of counter-invasion to establish monasteries throughout Europe. In the tradition of religious hermits obsessed with a rapture called *geilt* (the ecclesiastical equivalent of the *furor* of Celtic warriors), some would wander aimlessly to the sea and allow themselves to be borne out alone, perhaps to reach their visionary islands. The name for such wanderers was *peregrini.*

Some of them, perhaps Brendan and his crew, may have reached the tip of Newfoundland. Scholars long believed that the Brendan voyage was mere fantasy, given the fairly primitive state of shipbuilding at that time; but in 1977 and 1978, a group of young adventurers led by Tim Severin proved that it could have been accomplished. Using a nine-metre hide-covered boat modelled on the light *currachs,* the canoes of western Ireland, and adhering faithfully to medieval materials and workmanship, Severin and his crew sailed to Newfoundland in two seasons, crossing from the Hebrides to the Faroes, then to Iceland, wintering in Reykjavik, and then proceeding the following spring across the Denmark and Davis Straits to Newfoundland. The flexible boat of oak, ash, and leather bore them magnificently through the perilous ice of spring. Their landfall was Peckford Island, slightly to the south of the Strait

of Belle Isle; however, depending on the drift of the currents and the whim of the winds, it could just as easily have been 100 miles on either side.

Some theorists contend that Celtic mariners coasted far down the eastern seaboard, and so account for the inscribed stones, "observatories," and phallic monuments similar to those raised throughout Celtic Europe that have been found as far south as Massachusetts. In many cases the inscriptions on these mysterious monuments resemble an ancient Irish-Celtic script called Ogham, a complex system of dots and lines arranged in clusters and at various angles.

One such inscribed stone lies at the entry to the Gulf, on the north side of St. Lunaire Bay. Named by Breton fishermen, the bay has harboured a venerable succession of merchantmen and warships, for it provides an anchorage both safe and beautiful. Residents still turn up clay pipes and other oddments in their gardens. In a few fathoms beneath the cliffs on the north shore lie the barnacled cannons of some forgotten wreck.

High in the hills above those cannons, nestled in a grassy saddle criss-crossed by cowpaths, lies the curious boulder. It is about three metres in diameter, roughly round, and encrusted with lichens. Truncated black spruce curl around it, seeking shelter from the wind. On its western flank are yellowing platter-sized patches of what appears to be concrete, and scratched into these softer patches are the stick-like letters. They have been there as long as local memory. There are many explanations for them, including fakery; but it is at least feasible that they were made by voyaging Irish sometime before the year 500.

Standing at this place in the evening, gazing down on the rippling silver and black of St. Lunaire Bay, one wants to believe that the Celts did indeed come here, and that their questing spirit found at last a tranquillity to match that of their homeland. If the stone at St. Lunaire is authentic, then in time more evidence of the Celtic presence will be found at the entrance to the Gulf.

By the eleventh century the Norse had arrived. The Norse, supreme mariners whose very poetry holds the swells and crests of the sea:

Splashing oars raced
shield rang on shield
cutting the waves
farther and farther
iron rattled
as the Vikings rowed,
at the King's command,
the fleet sped on.

When the crested waves
crashed on the keels
was the boom of surf
of Kolga's sister
the sound that came
that breaks on rocks ...

NEAR RIVIERE AU TONNERRE, QUEBEC

CHALEUR BAY, NEAR BELLDUNE, NEW BRUNSWICK

HARRINGTON HARBOUR, QUEBEC

The first to reach Newfoundland might have rounded Cape Bauld in one of the sinewy dragon-prowed vessels from which they had ravaged the rivers of Europe, but this is unlikely. The dragonships were unsuitable for long-range seafaring, and there is little chance that experienced mariners would put out on the high seas in any craft with so little shelter and freeboard. Probably the earliest crossings to North America were from Norse colonies in Greenland, and were made in doughty merchant ships called *knorrir.*

Like the famous longship (and the intermediate form known as the *karv,* of which the Gokstad ship is an example), a knorr was of lapstreak, or clinker, construction. The spaces between its oaken planks were caulked with cords of grease-soaked hair. The steering oar hung on the right side – the starboard – and a single fabric squaresail reinforced with leather gathered the wind. All three types of Norse vessel were of very shallow draft (the average knorr drew only five feet), and all three were "alive" in the water, having sufficient resiliency to yield and twist under the pressures of the seas. Unlike the others, however, the knorr was designed for the open ocean. It had high freeboard and half-decking, and it was comparatively large, often reaching over thirty metres. Manned by a crew of about fifteen, the typical trading knorr carried two boats which, like the mother ship, could be either rowed or sailed.

On such a knorr, a group of colonists from Greenland reached the Strait of Belle Isle one spring day about the year 1000. Haggard and stiff after days of cold food, cold spray, and cramped quarters, they would have lined the rail to gaze at the coast behind its skirt of ice. Here was the rich land they had heard about. They would have watched eagerly as the crew altered course, swinging southward around Quirpon Island and the reefs of Foirou, and then down between Big and Little Sacred Islands and into a little cove off Épaves Bay. The big knorr would have ground gently on the sandy bottom, the crew would drop the squaresail, the steering oar would be swung safely inboard, and the colonists would splash ashore with their few head of cattle.

Behind the beach, a broad meadow greeted them. To the north, the low point where the village of L'Anse aux Meadows now lies curved into the sea, backed by the Sacred Islands, Verte Island, and Cape Artimon. Ahead, behind a boreal fringe, lay the rocky uplands out of which a fresh stream meandered through the meadows. To the south rose a craggy ridge from whose summit it was possible to see far out beyond the islands and, on a clear day, beyond Cape Bauld itself.

Perhaps Viking scouts had already built crude shelters to greet the colonists. If so they would have been sod, winter-worn but brightened by the profusion of flowers – iris, cloudberry, bunchberry, potentilla, partridgeberry, and cranberry – surrounding them and bedecking their roofs. If the time was right, spawning salmon would be so thick in Black Duck Creek that they could be scooped out by hand, fresh for supper. In the banks of that same creek, the settlers would find deposits of bog iron which they would laboriously smelt and craft into weapons and implements.

We do not know the names of these settlers, or how long they stayed, or what became of them. Even the assumption that they were Norse is based on tenuous evidence: the shape of their houses, the presence of the smithy, various bits of iron, a ring-headed bronze stickpin probably used to fasten a cloak, and a donut-shaped spindle-whorl of the type used by Norse women. It is remarkably little; and yet, taken together, it seems enough. We shall probably never know with certainty that this hamlet on the dark coast was actually Leifsbudir, the place that Leif Ericksson took for himself in the land he named Vinland, or whether it was Thorfinn Karlsefni's Straumfiord. It matters little which Norse freebooter named the place. What matters is that Europeans wintered here 1,000 years ago, resisted the aroused skraelings, and climbed the ridges to seek the spring-time sails of countrymen.

L'Anse aux Meadows is a magical place. It is good to walk there among the grassed mounds where buildings once stood, and along meandering Black Duck Creek to the place where it fans out across the beach. It is good to climb up the south ridge where cairns stand like sentinels brooding on the sea. Who built those cairns? Were they left by James Cook when he surveyed Sacred Bay in 1764, or did he, too, wonder about their origins while he "fixed Flaggs"?

The Norse likely inhabited L'Anse aux Meadows for no more than twenty years before emboldened skraelings, loosening ties with the mother colonies, and attrition by disease and accident forced the survivors to return to Greenland. Then again, perhaps they did not leave at all. Perhaps they were finally overwhelmed by raiders slipping down the surrounding slopes in the dusk. Perhaps they left their bones at L'Anse aux Meadows to be scattered by tides and animals. Or perhaps they came to an accommodation with the skraelings at last, joining in their hunting when the spring knorrs from Greenland failed to come, mingling with them in other bays and shelters far from L'Anse aux Meadows. Perhaps the legacy of those lost colonists rests in the genes of blue-eyed Eskimos.

Within a few generations, the Norse colony in Greenland was itself abandoned. Ice slid south, choking fiords. Mother Norway, riddled by Black Death, turned inward, losing seaways to the Hanseatic League and later to the upstart Bristol merchants. Norse songs and sagas died away, and the people who for so long had held their world in fear would themselves fall victim to inexorable new forces.

Once "discovered," the Strait of Belle Isle and the inland sea to the south of it never faded from European memory. It is impossible to believe that the Gulf was free of the European presence until it was rediscovered by the Corte-Reals, Cabot, and Cartier in the early 1500s. Bold but illiterate adventurers leave few records. Memories of the salmon, the seals, the cod, and the whales of the Gulf would have lingered among such mariners willing to risk a summer for a handsome profit in the fall. Basque whalers

OVERLEAF: GROSSE ILE, MAGDALEN ISLANDS, QUEBEC

were working in the Labrador Sea as early as 1420, and the Andreas de Bianco map of 1436 shows the "Isla de Stokafixa" (Cod Island) in Newfoundland's location. The fact that it was known to be an island is significant, for it means that fishermen were navigating the Cabot Strait, and it is reasonable to assume, therefore, that at least the northern coasts of the Gulf had been largely explored.

If the mouth of the St. Lawrence River was known in the 1400s, Spaniards probably brought the first descriptions of it back to Europe. Spaniards were whalers. While the French Basques had access to large quantities of salt from the south of France and therefore tended to exploit the codfish market, the Spaniards had the iron required for harpoons, barrel-hoops, and the try-cauldrons in which blubber was rendered to oil. Consequently, the French Basques probably fished the rich Grand Banks and coasted the eastern side of Newfoundland, while the Spaniards hunted whales inside the Gulf itself. Remnants of ancient try-works have been found as far west as La Malbaie, and as far north as Labrador. Basque captains were tough entrepreneurs, and although their boats often co-operated with each other in hauling whales to shore for the flensing, many squabbles over ownership led to litigation in Spain.

Whalers usually set out in July and returned in January, although sometimes they were caught for a year in Labrador ice. For their shore installations – habitations, warehouses, and try-works – the Basques carried to "Terra Nova" quantities of brick-red roofing tile, pieces of which can still be found along the north shore.

From above the settlements, on the hills of Red Bay, Pinware, St. Modest, and Blanc Sablon, lookouts watched for the spouts of browsing whales. Killing was perilous, for it involved slipping up beside the leviathans in small boats and driving home harpoons, usually two. If the whale sounded, carefully coiled line was paid out from tubs, and the tense wait began until the animal breached again. If the whale swam across the surface, the little boats might be pulled along for miles in what was later called "a Nantucket sleigh-ride." Eventually, if the whale did not break loose, it would be killed with a lance-stroke into its vitals.

Cadavers were then laboriously tugged to the harbours for butchering in the sloping meadows above high tide. Hundreds of small pieces of blubber were flensed out for boiling. Stripped corpses were sometimes set adrift in the currents of the Strait, but the amount of bleached and ancient whalebone remaining in the meadows is testimony that many were left to rot. Immense skulls gaze from eyeless sockets at the sea, and huge vertebrae lie tumbled amidst the profusion of flowers and grass.

In the frenzy of high season at a Basque whaling port, the stench of boiling and rotting whale meat must have been appalling. In an average year in the sixteenth century, 20,000 barrels of oil went from the Gulf to Europe, destined to be turned into lubricants, candles, and fuel for lamps.

As the century ended, however, Basque suzerainty in the Gulf crumbled under growing competition and other factors. The disaster of the Armada in 1588 dealt a heavy blow to Spain's maritime economy. Venture capital vanished. Moreover, the English and the Dutch had begun hunting whales in their own coastal waters, and the fresh influx of cheaper oil ended the Spanish monopoly. A few whalers persevered (thirty-eight Basques stayed at Red Bay over the winter of 1604-5), but within a few years their outports decayed and newcomers either built upon the ruins or sailed obliviously past them.

No maps of the Gulf from the early sixteenth century have yet come to light. The La Cosa map of 1500 reveals extensive knowledge of the Caribbean and the northern coasts of South America, but "Terra Nova" is comparatively undetailed. The region is marked with five British flags and described as the "sea discovered by the English." The mapmaker obviously knew of John Cabot's 1497 voyage to the Gulf, but he knew little of where Cabot had gone and what he had discovered.

All regions have their shadowy figures, part mythological, part real, skirting the edges of history. In the record of the Gulf, John Cabot is such a figure. We know that he was an Italian, probably a Genoese, and that his name is an Anglicized form of Cabotto (or Chiabotto, or Bagoto, or even Talbot), meaning *coaster*. We know that after a chequered career in Venice he moved his family to Bristol, where there was an active trade with Iceland and where voyages of exploration had already been launched in 1491 and 1492. Sheriff Richard Amerike was one of Cabot's backers, but most important to him was the personal interest of Henry VII, who regretted missing his chance to finance Columbus. On 5 March 1496, Henry issued this permission to "wel-beloved John Cabot, citizen of Venice, to Lewis, Sebastian, and Santius, sonnes of the said John, full and free authority, leave and power to saile to all parts, countries and seas of the East, of the West, and of the North, under our banners and ensignes ... to seek out, discover and finde whatsoever isles, countries, regions or provinces of the heathen and infidels, in what part of the world soever they be, which before this time, have beene unknowen to all Christians."

Cabot was to pay Henry one-fifth "of the gain of all fruits, profits, gaines and commodities growing of such navigation."

Cabot's vessel was the *Mathew*, a trim little caravel of fifty tuns (that is, capable of carrying fifty tuns, or standard barrels). She was slightly smaller than Columbus's *Nina*. She probably carried four or five sails on three masts, and a crew of twenty. She crossed the Atlantic in thirty-five days, remarkably good time, considering that in the 1800s a crossing of two months was not unusual.

Beyond these facts we know little of Cabot. It may be that he touched Cape Breton and ventured into the Gulf (or perhaps made landfall in the vicinity of Newfoundland's Cape Degrat) and that from there he sailed south and turned back for Europe at Cape Race. Wherever he had gone and

MONT LOUIS, GASPÉ PENINSULA, QUEBEC

whatever he had seen, Cabot was convinced that if he probed only a little farther he would gather oriental riches.

Impetus for further exploration came from Angra in the Azores. Labrador may have acquired its name from one João Fernandes, an Azorean landowner and farmer (*lavrador*) who helped to finance a voyage to Greenland in 1500. His company called Greenland "Tiera del Lavrador," and cartographers later shifted "Labrador" to the west, having restored the Norse name to Greenland.

Such shifting of names was not the first in the Gulf's history. In fact, the Gulf of St. Lawrence itself was probably named by cartographical accident, for Jacques Cartier gave the name "St. Lawrence" to only a small bay on the north shore. His name for Miscou Point, "Cap d'Espérance," which he conferred in the belief that he had found a passage west, eventually drifted westward itself and mutated, becoming Gaspé's Cap d'Espoir. Even Acadia derived its name from Verranzano's name for Virginia: "Arcadie," the mythical land of ease and plenty, itself named after the bountiful region of ancient Greece.

While João Fernandes was venturing towards Greenland another Azorean, Caspar Corte-Real, was also heading west. After an initial voyage in 1500, he launched a more ambitious fleet of three ships the following year. Two of these returned to the Azores bearing Indians ("clothed in Beestes skynnes ... and ate raw fflessh and were rude in their demeanure as Beestes"), but Corte-Real's own vessel continued westward and was never seen again. The Gulf consumed him, the first of its victims whose name we know. How far did he and his crew go? Did they reach the mouth of the St. Lawrence and, beguiled by the broad fresh water, continue inland as the frosts came and the sea thickened inexorably behind them?

The following year, Corte-Real's brother set out in search of him with two ships, and in an ironic mirroring of events he, too, dropped from history while the accompanying ship returned safely to Portugal, having sailed up the western coast of Newfoundland and named several bays.

All these voyages doubtless confirmed in Europe Cabot's report that codfish abounded in this new sea. "They somtymes stayed his shippes." For his part, Sebastian Cabot wove fanciful tales about how the cod were scooped from the shallows by wading bears. An awed retainer of the Duke of Milan wrote, in 1497, "The sea there is swarming with fish, which can be taken not only with the net, but in baskets ..." Soon after the Corte-Reals' ventures, the first records of profitable voyages (sometimes two per year by the same ships and crews) begin to appear in the ledgers of Honfleur, Le Havre, St. Malo, Brest, and La Rochelle. Eager to share this new wealth, Norman, Breton, and Gascon captains were probing regularly into the Gulf in the first decades of the 1500s and bringing back reports wondrously transformed with distance and repeated tellings.

The fish which inspired all this activity is extremely unprepossessing. *Gadus callarias Linnaeus* has one of the most doleful expressions of all species; it looks like a natural victim. Although the etymology of its common name, cod, is uncertain, it is also the old English word for male genitalia.

It is a prolific fish. A gravid 100-centimetre female will lay three million eggs. These float free to the surface where, after a circling mating dance, the female leads the male above and through them, inducing the release of sperm. Fertilized eggs drift free; unfertilized ones drop to the bottom and die.

Cod move in vast schools. Although they prefer to feed on the bottom, tasting prospective morsels with the filament barbel on their chins, they will also eat other fish, rising to the surface if necessary. Their principal food is herring, capelin, squid, jellyfish, crabs, worms, molluscs, and smaller cod.

In the Gulf they are found in shallow littoral waters and on the four major banks: the Whittle Bank between Anticosti and the Strait of Belle Isle; the Orphan Bank off Gaspé Bay; the Bradelle Bank off Chaleur Bay; and the shallows around the Magdalens. They prefer to live and breed in a specific gravity of 1.024, which is that of the open sea, and the lowered salinity caused by the influx of fresh water makes the Gulf less attractive as a spawning ground than eastern Newfoundland. Their average size in the Gulf is between two and twenty-five pounds, and they grow smaller as one proceeds north. Sixty-pounders were fairly common at the turn of the century, and one is on record at 211 pounds. Exploitation of the cod schools has been systematically reducing both size and numbers. They are caught either in nets or by *jigging*, snagging them on unbaited hooks.

The two basic methods of curing fish have remained little changed over the centuries. At sea they were caught, cleaned, and salted on board the ships, a method which required speed and plentiful amounts of salt. Fortunate ships could make a swift catch and return home without touching land. The other technique, the one used by land-based fishermen, was to clean the fish at the end of each day on raised docks called *stages*, and then to spread the split fish to dry on pebble beaches. Such beaches, highly coveted in sheltered locations, were called *grèves*. The most desirable were those composed of stones large enough to permit circulation but not too large to make walking uncomfortable; a good example is the Grand Grève in Gaspé Bay. Those fishermen who reached the grounds too late to gain access to the best beaches built brushwood drying tables in other locations.

Cod caught in winter and dried in the frost were called *stockfish*. Summer-dried cod from Newfoundland were called *poorjohn* by the English and *labourd* or *haberdine* by the Basques. On European markets, salted fish were worth about twice as much as dried fish.

When they arrived at the stages, cod were pulled from the baskets or barrels by their eyes, their throats were slit gill-to-gill, and their bellies sliced lengthwise. Livers were plucked out and kept for their valuable oil, but the guts and heads were dropped into the sea or tossed to the dogs. Finally,

ABOVE: "UNCLE" DAN BOBBIT, BUILDER OF THE LAST SCHOONER, WITH HIS WIFE ROSE; HARRINGTON HARBOUR, QUEBEC

OPPOSITE: STANHOPE BEACH, PRINCE EDWARD ISLAND

the backbones were extracted and the split fish taken by wheelbarrow to the *store*, where they were lightly salted and stacked to await their spreading on the tables or *flakes*. As the weather changed and the rains came and went, the fish were gathered and spread several times. This drying process, which took the cod into marketable condition, was called *making fish*. It was and is tedious, dirty labour; but it was the work on which the first commercial empire in Canada was founded, the main work of the earliest colonists.

The Harrington Islands huddle against the north shore of the Gulf just south of the Strait of Belle Isle. They are part of the archipelago of Mecatina, a sprawling network of islands, islets, and shoals stretching from Tête-à-la-Baleine northward. They have been worn into smooth, whaleback shapes by ice and seas, polished by rains and incessant winds. Stunted herbage crouches in their crevices. Snow lingers into July. Above the tidelines, stubborn colonies of lichen fleck the pink-brown rock flanks with pale green, spreading an inch per century.

Unless one has been born to this place, or has grown to love the dark moods of the sea, the Harringtons are one of the most desolate places on earth. Even today, despite the little community nestled in their securest harbour, to be marooned on the Harringtons at certain seasons would mean death. Yet here, in 1542, on one of the group then called Ile des Démons, two women and a man were abandoned by their comrades. In order to understand how such a thing could happen, we must go back eight years to 1534, and the entry into the Gulf of its principal explorer, Jacques Cartier.

A foolish nineteenth-century painting shows Cartier bedecked with lace and velvet, sword and dagger, staring pensively over the rail of a ship about to sail into Atlantic reefs. No contemporary portrait of the man exists. We know little about him except that he was probably over forty when he accepted the commission of His Most Christian Majesty, Francis I, for an exploratory voyage in 1534. He seems to have been well known to Jean Le Veneur, Abbé of Mont St. Michel and Grand Almoner of France, who recommended him to Francis as a man well qualified "by virtue of his voyages to Brazil and the New Land ... to lead ships in the discovery of new territories in the New World."

A Breton, Cartier would have grown up with the sea in his blood. He would never have been far from the sea, from its winds and odours. As a child he would have watched Breton farmers ploughing their fields in the traditional undulating patterns of the ocean, and he would have heard the tales of the legendary lost city of Ys – cursed to sink by Satan because he could not equal its splendour – whose cathedral bells still tolled beneath the sea. He would have stared in wonder at the Neolithic relics entangled in fishermen's nets, and he would have mused beside the strange stone monuments, the menhirs and dolmens, lowering in the Breton hills above the sea. Who had raised them? How long ago?

NEAR L'ANSE À VALLEAU, GASPÉ PENINSULA, QUEBEC

Did those people come from the sea and return to it? Were their cities undiscovered still, somewhere to the west?

On 20 April 1534, Cartier led two ships and sixty-one men westward from St. Malo. We do not know the names of the ships or the men. The crossing was swift and routine; he seems to have known his initial destination precisely. He touched Newfoundland first at Bonavista Bay, then proceeded to Funk Island for the customary supply of fresh-slaughtered auks, and then to the Strait of Belle Isle, which he knew as Chateaux Bay. Probably he paused in the excellent harbour provided by Ile du Bassin at Bradore, where a large cod fishery had been established.

The arc of the great beach at Bradore sweeps south to the little river called Ruisseau des Belles Amours, which tumbles in stages out of the hills until it curls into the sea. On the plateaus above the bay, awesome boulders lie strewn like Titan playthings.

It is tempting to imagine Cartier drawn by these stones so like the megaliths of Carnac, hiking up the glacier track that parallels the river until he reached the summit and could gaze to the south, down a ragged coast dotted with pale green icebergs, and far inland over the endless, windswept plains and ponds. Empty, empty. Perhaps here the staunch Breton, pestered by clouds of blackflies, came to the conclusion that was confirmed farther south: " ... the land should not be called the New Land, being composed of stones and horrible rugged rocks; for along the whole of the north shore I did not see one cart-load of earth ... this is the land God gave to Cain." Later, however, Cartier would come to fertile lands that pleased him more.

While his ships were being reprovisioned in Brest, a town in Bonne Espérance Bay a few leagues to the south of Bradore, Cartier explored farther by longboat. He encountered the first Indian *mishwaps* at Shekatika, and described their inhabitants:

> There are people on this coast whose bodies are fairly well formed but they are wild and savage folk. They wear their hair tied up on the top of their heads like a handful of twisted hay, with a nail or something of the sort passed through the middle, and into it they weave a few bird's feathers. They clothe themselves with the furs of animals, both men as well as women; but the women are wrapped up more closely and snugly in their furs; and they have a belt about their waists. They paint themselves with certain tan colours.

From Shekatika, Cartier crossed to the west coast of Newfoundland. Halfway over he noted "a large cape doubled one part above the other, and on this account we named it Cape Double." These were two peaks of the Highlands of St. John at the north end of Ingornachoix Bay In the shadow of

NEAR LA POINTE, CAPE BRETON ISLAND, NOVA SCOTIA

NEAR BIG BROOK, STRAIT OF BELLE ISLE, NEWFOUNDLAND

these hills, close to the ancient aboriginal settlements of Port aux Choix, he touched Newfoundland.

From there he sailed south, beset by foul weather, leaving a string of French names for visible landmarks and bays. Off Cap Anguille he angled southwest towards the centre of the Gulf and raised the Magdalens, the beautiful windswept islands that would later become the grave of hundreds of ships and men. The northernmost of this group Cartier named Brion after his patron, Philippe de Chabot, Seigneur de Brion and Admiral of France.

After the rocks of Newfoundland and the north shore, Brion seemed a pastoral paradise to Cartier, abundant in wild herbs, berries, and roses. He found foxes inhabiting it, and bears. Here also he saw walrus for the first time, "great beasts, like large oxen, which have two tusks in their jaw like elephant's tusks and swim about in the water." He saw thousands as he sailed down the west coast of the Magdalens, for the beaches there were among their favourite breeding grounds.

Assuming that the Magdalens were a promontory of the south shore, Cartier headed southwest, skirted Cascumpque and Miramichi Bays, rounded Miscou, and entered Chaleur Bay where he lingered eight days, trading with Indians. He met a different group to the north, in Gaspé Bay, and realizing that they had knowledge of routes west, he did everything possible to make friends with them. Eventually, he took away the two sons of the chief, Donnaconna, obviously intending to have interpreters when he returned the following year.

Mistaking Gaspé Passage for a dead end, he sailed straight to Anticosti, rounded Heath Point at the eastern end of the island, and turned west between Anticosti's north shore and the mainland. He was now sure he had found a major passage west, but winds and tides were against him and the season was late. To probe farther would have meant the risk of wintering in this land of Cain. So, on Saturday 1 August, in the vicinity of the Mingan Islands, the companies of both ships assembled on Cartier's vessel and, considering "that as the storms usually began at that season in Newfoundland, and we were still a long way off, and did not know the dangers that lay between these two places ...," voted to turn back.

Going home, Cartier made only one stop between the Mingans and Blanc Sablon – at Natashquan. Then, in two long tacks, he crossed deep water to his familiar Cape Double, and thence to Blanc Sablon.

For the moment the Orient had eluded him; but as the last islands of the New World faded above the wake of his ship, Cartier must have been content with the promise of another season and with what he had achieved. He had proven La Grande Baie to be larger and more various than anyone had anticipated, and he had found a promising passage to the west. Tangible awards awaited him in France, but more important than these, as he listened throughout that winter to the rolling of the winter sea at St. Malo and slowly deciphered the guttural descriptions of his Indian guests, were the bright prospects of new lands and new peoples west of Natashquan.

RAINSTORM, JACQUES CARTIER PASSAGE, GULF OF ST. LAWRENCE

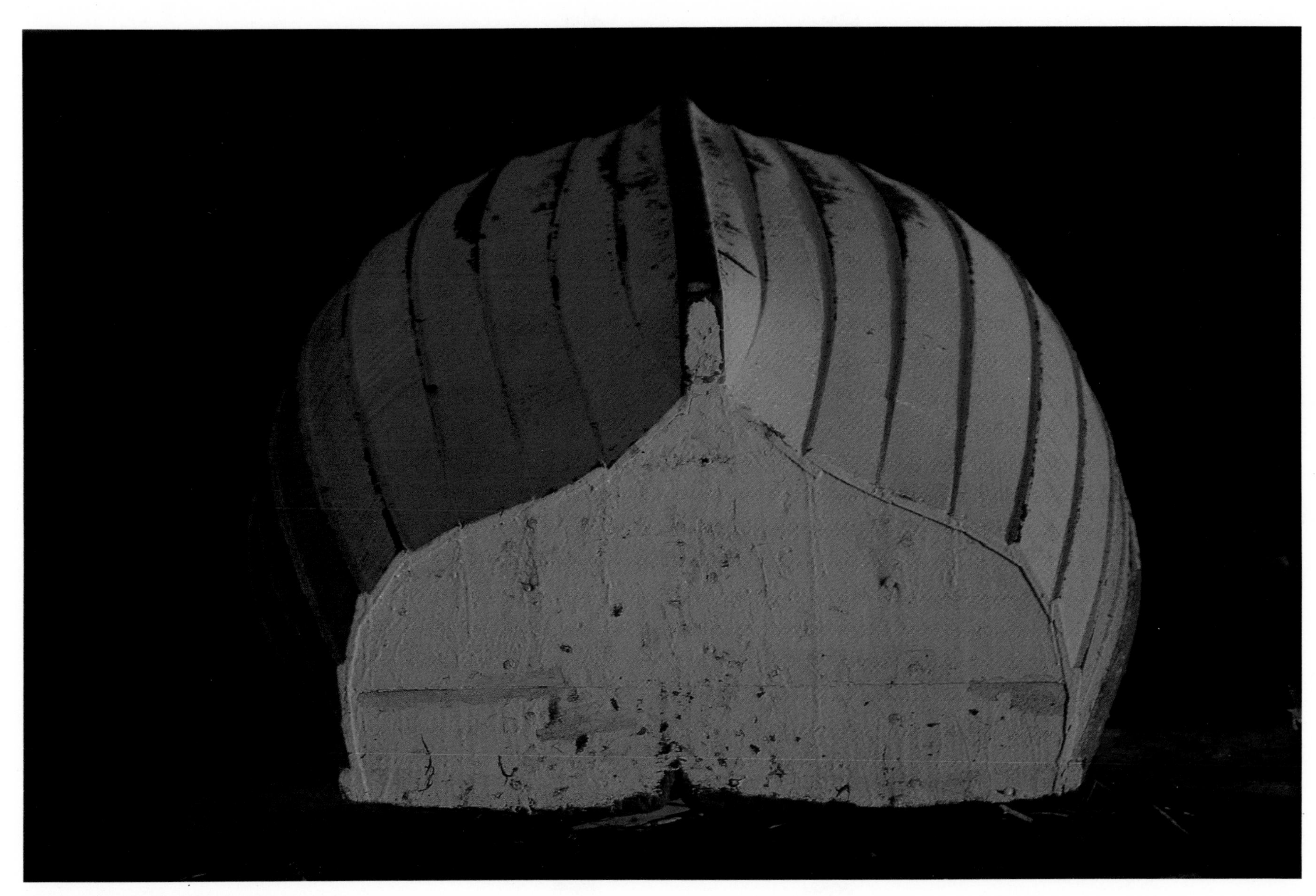

ABOVE: CANÔT, LONGUE POINTE DE MINGAN, QUEBEC

OPPOSITE: FORILLON NATIONAL PARK, GASPÉ BAY, QUEBEC

The next year Cartier would follow the north shore directly to the Mingans. On this voyage he would have three ships: *Grande Hermyne, Petite Hermyne,* and *Hemerillon.* He would take shelter in a small bay behind Ile Ste. Geneviève on 10 August, St. Lawrence's Day, and he would name that little bay after the saint. Within a few years the name would extend to the river and, by 1569, on Mercator's map, to the Gulf itself.

On that second voyage, Cartier would journey inland to a place called Hochelaga, where his progress would be stopped by rapids. He would winter among the Indians, and he would leave the bodies of twenty-five French, dead of scurvy and other diseases. On his homeward passage through the Gulf, he would head to the south of Anticosti, this time sailing right through the cloudy mountains that had deterred him a year and a half earlier. He would discover that "Les Araines," the Magdalens, were an archipelago, and he would confirm his suspicion that a passage lay through the Cabot Strait, thus proving Newfoundland to be an island. By July 1536, Jacques Cartier had traced the lineaments of La Grande Baie.

Cartier's voyages established the Gulf as a geographic entity. The impetus of discovery would henceforth push west beyond it, along glittering inland waterways, and for later voyagers the Gulf would be either a portal to the sea or a receptacle, the first stage in the gentle process of being enfolded by Canada. The intricacies of its harbours and rivers, the riches of its soils and shoals, the threats and irritations of its reefs and inhabitants – all of these, in the subsequent centuries of settlement, remained to be discovered by trial and error, and by that residue of shared experience which is history.

Cartier's work brought the odour of fresh wealth to Francis I, "le roi grand nez," but it was obvious to him that the new land could be held against Spanish and English claims only by colonists. Accordingly, in 1541, he gave his consent and support to the first official colonizing expedition in Canadian history. It would be led by François de La Rocque de Le Roberval, a colleague of Cartier and a Protestant with an impressive military record. Roberval's powers were to be absolute. The expedition from its inception was apparently to have a high moral and evangelical tone, for Francis himself had grown genuinely devout. As an athletic and handsome youth, he had been noted for his warm reception of ladies, one of whom gave him syphilis. Mercury, the cure of the day, had ravaged his nervous system. Another disease in 1538 had left him with a severe stutter, and in later years he acquired a rancorous abscess; his reign in its later stages was fraught with personal as well as state afflictions. As he became less attractive physically he grew more pious and intolerant, and the appointment of the splenetic Roberval to weld together his Canadian enterprise may have been a result of this change in character.

PERCÉ ROCK, GASPÉ PENINSULA, QUEBEC

LIGHTHOUSE DETAIL, MISCOU ISLAND, NEW BRUNSWICK

VIEUX PHARE, POINTE DES MONTS, QUEBEC

OVERLEAF: SURF AT POINTE RICHE, NEWFOUNDLAND

Roberval received his commission from the king in January 1541, and he and Cartier worked henceforth under the diligent eyes of Spanish spies, one of whom reported that their expedition consisted of 1,500 people. Many of these emigrants were convicts and conscripts. Cartier's contingent sailed first, and in the summer and autumn of 1541 established Charlesbourg Royal near present-day Montreal. Roberval followed in the spring of 1542 only to meet Cartier at St. Jean, Newfoundland, returning after a disastrous winter. Cartier refused to accompany his commander back across the Gulf and into the river, and went straight home to France, believing that he had discovered incalculable wealth in gold and diamonds. Committed to the settlement and chafing under Cartier's insubordination, Roberval continued around Cape Bauld and down the Strait of Belle Isle, towards the Harrington Islands.

Together with the convicts on board Roberval's ships were several members of the French aristocracy, including some of Roberval's relatives. One of these was Marguerite de La Roque. Off the Harringtons, Roberval learned that this lady had formed a liaison during the voyage with a young man, and that this indiscretion had occurred with the knowledge of her servant, Damienne. Roberval immediately hove to, had a boat provisioned, and put the two women ashore on one of the islands. Before the ships were underway, however, the girl's lover joined the women by either commandeering a boat or swimming ashore. The three castaways then watched Roberval's ships hoist sail and leave them to their fate.

Even for a man of his temperament, Roberval's judgement seems harsh. Why, if they were lovers and wished to be married, did he not simply marry them? That was within his power. It is true that the standards of the time were stern and Roberval had to impose strict discipline on this mixed group of settlers. Through the winter he would have one colonist hanged, several placed in irons, and several more whipped, both men and women. Perhaps the hapless Marguerite was selected as an early example to the others; perhaps she and Damienne had aggravated him during the voyage; perhaps the young man was far beneath her station, perhaps even a convict.

That Marguerite survived is amazing; that she survived alone is miraculous. The first winter her lover died, leaving her pregnant. The next year she lost both her child and Damienne. Yet she endured, gathering berries and roots, catching fish, occasionally killing birds and other game with the arquebuses Roberval had left her. She killed three bears (one of them apparently a polar bear), and she protected herself from the demons which howled about her on winter nights. She came to know wolves well, and migrating seals, and wolverines, and the ghastly cries of great cats, like babes in torment. She kept her watchfires ready, and in the spring of 1544, when she had been stranded for almost two and one-half years, she caught the attention of astonished fishermen. She returned with them to France and to her home in Picardy, the first European known to have lived more than one winter in Canada.

LEFT: NEAR THE MOUTH OF THE CHETICAMP RIVER, CAPE BRETON ISLAND, NOVA SCOTIA

RIGHT: ETANG DU NORD, MAGDALEN ISLANDS, QUEBEC

Meanwhile, Roberval's colony had failed, together with official French designs on what was believed to be the fabulously rich "Kingdom of Saguenay." As for Cartier, he was disillusioned and humiliated to discover that the riches he believed he had brought to France were nothing but a last joke on him, the land's equivalent of Chief Donnaconna's duping tales. The "leaves of fine gold as thick as a man's nayle" were only pyrite, and the "diamants the most faire pollished and excellently cut" were nothing but quartz. Like the Indians he had abducted, Cartier never returned to Canada. He died in an epidemic at St. Malo on 1 September 1557. His legacy lies in the maps and in the French names that line the Gulf.

Through the sixteenth century, a host of mapmakers kept Cartier's basic cartography of the Gulf and the River St. Lawrence. Desliens, Descaliers, Vallard, and Mercator, as well as several speculative publishers and anonymous mapmakers who pirated charts with only slight changes, all used Cartier's nomenclature. In 1601, G. Levasseur replaced Cartier's Huron-Iroquois names with Algonkian ones – *gaspay, natistcoti, tadoucaq, quebecq* – and added new French ones: Ile St. Jean, Ile Bonaventure, Le Bic. Through the seventeenth century the major mapmakers of New France would do their work: Champlain, Jumeau, and De Meulles. And with the precise French and British Admiralty charts of the eighteenth and nineteenth centuries, the shorelines of the Gulf would be fully traced, its depths plumbed.

The men who made these maps were the consolidators of a mathematical way of viewing the Gulf. Hydrography is a matter of patient and precise assemblage. The myriad placements of the transit; the plumb-line repeatedly dropping; the leadsman continually calling out the depths; the lamp-lit tracings as little by little the puzzle fits itself together – these require a mind that is not only that of the mystic, the adventurer, the gambler. They require someone willing to take inventories and produce sums. On such work the European thrust to the west proceeded through the Gulf. Surveyors precede progress. Subtly, ominously, they are also the agents whereby the land is first contained, then in stages diminished, degraded, and disregarded, through the methodical process of having its mysteries dispelled. Even if one views maps as expressions of trust and friendship, it is possible to know too well, to assist too thoroughly.

The work of mapmakers leaves as little as possible to the imagination, and it is the imagination that the winds, surfs, fogs, and reefs of the Gulf specifically invite. It is good to see once again in the mind's eye a tiny Celtic, or Norse, or Basque, or Breton craft cautiously feeling its way down the coast towards some great new knowledge, its crew united in curiosity.

As the seasonal European fisheries grew, Micmac and Montagnais families more and more often returned to traditional summering beaches to find them occupied. White strangers were there, landing from pestilent ships in the offing. They had hollow sticks that could kill at great distance, and fire-lances that screeched like demons overhead. But they also offered wonderful goods: knives, axes, adzes, and chisels – all vastly superior to the Indians' own chert and copper implements; pots of the same splendid metal; warm, bright blankets; silver and magical glass beads to gleam against a woman's skin. All of these wonders were available for a commodity the Indians had in abundance: furs.

The people in Chaleur Bay who came out in their canoes to wave furs at Cartier's ship had already learned what the French desired. As the years passed, the amount of surplus lynx, otter, marten, fox, mink, and beaver that they had formerly gathered for trade with neighbouring tribes would be increased for trade with the French: *micmac* means "ally." From their new friendship, both races believed that they were benefiting and, indeed, in some ways both were. But the cost to the Micmacs would be far, far more than the few skins agreed upon in single barters. The cost, finally, would be a culture.

The impact on native life was both economic and social. They began to spend more time gathering surplus furs for trade, and animal populations – the principal Indian resource base – were soon stressed and depleted. Barter between equals deteriorated to pathetic reliance. Sexual commerce swiftly added to the Montagnais and Micmac tribulations, producing both disease and pale offspring uncertain of their heritage, ignorant of ancestral skills. Besides venereal infections, measles, smallpox, whooping cough, influenza, and other ship-borne afflictions decimated populations. By the time the direction of events was obvious it was much too late; not only were the effects irreversible, but the white men were more numerous every year. They controlled the coasts.

Among the Malecite, halfbreeds became known as *malouidit*, "because the greater part of their fathers came from St. Malo." On the other side of the Gulf, an early nineteenth-century traveller made this comment on the coastal Montagnais: "Being enervated by their slothful habits, too free of indulgence in the use of spirituous liquors and in debaucheries of every kind, their minds are stupid, their persons diminutive, and their constitutions weak."

Political alignments among tribes also shifted; some chiefs or tribes benefited more than others from French assistance. But the most devastating effect of the inter-racial exchange was ideological. Breton technical superiority dealt the Indian cultures an initial blow which sent them reeling, and before they had recovered the priests had arrived. First the Recollets and then the Jesuits worked tirelessly, subtly, to undermine the Indians' vital pantheism, and to convert their belief in an animate universe into Christian idealism. They used all the devices at their disposal – bribery, threat, persuasion, kindness, and infinite patience – and they were terribly successful. They produced the converts whose photographs

LEFT: BOAT-BUILDING DETAIL, HARRINGTON HARBOUR, QUEBEC

RIGHT: BRACKLEY BEACH, PRINCE EDWARD ISLAND NATIONAL PARK

haunt the nineteenth century, lined up in their ties and dresses in front of churches, always unsmiling, looking exactly like what they were – the spruced-up victims of a disaster. *Papinachois*, they had been called once: "les gens qui rient."

As if the traders and blackrobes were not enough, a bewildering array of white chiefs soon began to find their way into the Gulf, full of conflicting orders, often openly hostile to each other. Faith in the *sachems* and *sagamos* having been lost, the question for the Indians became not so much, "Who, among all these governors is right?" but rather, "Who is most powerful and protective?" With that question they reached the final stages of debasement. The Montagnais and Micmac were the first to touch bottom, but they would not be the last. Cultures crumbled inexorably, tribe by tribe, as progress and development rolled up the St. Lawrence and into the new land. That Algonkian languages are still spoken around the Gulf is a tribute to the will of proud women, the ultimate protectors and nourishers of culture.

Because we cannot project ourselves into the minds of sixteenth-century Indians, we cannot know how they viewed the whites during the earliest stages of contact. Of course they themselves left no written records, and those left by white observers are either, like the Jesuits', filled with Christian rationalization and the desire to impress financial backers or, like the explorer-traders', laconic and detached. Reading the early accounts is like trying to see figures in a darkening forest. Rarely are there such flashes of clarity as this speech of a Micmac leader to some Frenchmen at Percé in the 1690s:

> Thou reproachest us, very inappropriately, that our country is a little hell in contrast with France, which thou comparest to a terrestrial paradise, inasmuch as it yields thee, so thou sayest, every kind of provision in abundance. Thou sayest of us also that we are the most miserable and most unhappy of all men, living without religion, without manners, without honour, without social order, and, in a word, without any rules, like beasts in our woods and our forests, lacking bread, wine, and a thousand other comforts which thou hast in superfluity in Europe.
>
> Well, my brother, if thou dost not yet know the real feelings which our Indians have towards thy country and towards all thy nation, it is proper that I inform thee at once.
>
> I beg thee to believe that, all miserable as we seem in thine eyes, we consider ourselves nevertheless much happier than thou in this, that we are very content with the little that we have; and believe also once and for all, I pray, that thou deceivest thyself

greatly if thou thinkest to persuade us that thy country is better than ours. For if France, as thou sayest, is a little terrestrial paradise, art thou sensible to leave it?

... Which of these two is the wisest and happiest – he who labours without ceasing and only obtains, and that with great trouble, enough to live on, or he who rests in comfort and finds all that he needs in the pleasure of hunting and fishing? ... Learn now, my brother, once and for all, because I must open to thee my heart: there is no Indian who does not consider himself infinitely more happy and more powerful than the French.

The white view of the Indian, on the other hand, is well recorded. They were *les sauvages*, dwellers of the woods, brutish, cruel, untrustworthy, obviously inferior. The dutiful would raise them to Christianity and civility; the unprincipled would exploit them. The Viking Thorvald's impetuous slaying of the first skraelings he met, and the various Breton and British kidnappings, foreshadowed the arrogance of generations of European businessmen, governors, and missionaries.

It is interesting to speculate what might have occurred had the European arrival been delayed long enough for the diplomatically sophisticated and powerful Iroquois Confederacy to have doubled or trebled in strength. Along the coast the white-comers might then have been faced by two formidable nations, the Huron-Iroquois and the Algonquins, linked in resistance.

A poignant Micmac tale from Prince Edward Island concentrates mythically the key elements in the white arrival. A young girl, so the story goes, had a dream in which she saw an island, bearing a man in rabbit skins and trees full of bear-like creatures, drifting towards her. Tribal shamans were perplexed by the dream until next day a ship appeared in the bay, its rigging full of bundled sailors, its surpliced priest reaching towards shore. In a few lines the little tale tells much, with its sense of inevitability, its shamanistic puzzlement and impotence, and its men like bears, the most venerated of Algonquin animals.

Nowhere was the onslaught against the Indians more ruthless than among the Beothuks in Newfoundland. The story reflects no credit on the English. Whatever their intentional or unwitting depredations in the Gulf, the French at least regarded les sauvages as human beings with souls, and not quarry for sport. There is no reason to believe that during their tenure of Newfoundland they regarded the Beothuks any differently. From the outset, however, the relations between English and Beothuk seemed destined to failure. When Sir Humphrey Gilbert took possession of all of Newfoundland for England in 1583, his second-in-command wrote: "In the South ports we found no inhabitants, which by all likelyhood have abandoned these coasts, the same being much frequented by Christians; but in the North are savages altogether harmless."

The Beothuks continued to be wary, and with very good reason if a letter written in 1612 gives any indication of how they were treated. The writer, John Guy, spent the winter of 1610-1611 with a small group in Conception Bay. While there, the British apparently established friendly relations with the Beothuks, and Guy gave a detailed account of their way of life. When the English departed, they arranged to meet the Beothuks at the same place the following spring. Unfortunately, another ship happened on the prearranged spot before Guy's. Its captain mistook the convivial display onshore for belligerence and ordered grapeshot fired into the massed Indians.

What began in error continued in earnest. Driven from ancestral coastal summering grounds, the Beothuks retreated to the interior of the island, with a social dislocation that can only be imagined. As the decades passed they were routinely killed by white and Micmac hunting parties, until an entire race had been exterminated. On 6 June 1829, the last of the Beothuks, a girl named Shawnadithit, died from tuberculosis in St. John's, and the long genocide was finished.

For all the Indians of the Gulf and the lower St. Lawrence River, the period following white contact was a time of terrible upheaval and uncertainty. European inroads and their attendant changes – social dislocation, ecological imbalance, shifting alliances and trade patterns – all must have contributed to an agony of which we have only the faintest inklings. Now and again hints of what happened to the Amerind fishers of the Gulf wink like distant campfires through a forest of official commissions and reports, but before they can be investigated they flicker out and vanish. By the time Champlain arrived in 1603, the Huron-Iroquois were altogether gone from the region, and the Gulf shores were loosely populated with shifting Algonquin bands.

From the middle of the sixteenth century, traders were pushing up the St. Lawrence and into the interior. By 1600, the fur trade had become an important part of the economy of France, and annual voyages were made solely to trade with the Indians who packed their winter catches down the big rivers that fed the Gulf. Around the mouths of these rivers, on beaches steaming in the summer sun and dotted by herons stalking their prey, the deals were struck. Most prized by the French was the fur of the beaver, a venerable and rather thick-witted creature found by the millions in Canada's streams and ponds. Beaver fur was ideal for felt, and skins taken directly off the Indians' backs were best, for a year's use as clothing would rub away the two-inch guard hairs and leave only the dense, *cotonné* mat of fur. Such skins became known as *castor gras d'hiver*, and they made, as the traveller Lahontan reported, "the finest Down in the world."

GASPÉ BAY, QUEBEC

Through the 1500s, however, fur remained second to cod in economic importance, and the close competition for good beaches on which to dry the cod catch led to the building of shore installations and to the leaving of caretakers to protect them over the winter. Joined in time by women and children, many of these winterers found the wild coasts more congenial than pastoral Brittany. They stayed. They planted gardens and fenced them with woven brush. In time, they raised livestock. They became the first real settlers; through them the French held the Gulf, and through the Gulf, Canada.

During the late 1500s, England did not contest France's ownership. On the edges of the Gulf, Humphrey Gilbert claimed all of Newfoundland shortly before he was "swallowed up of the sea." Frobisher, Davis, and nine other English explorers nudged their little caravels deep into Arctic ice, and Raleigh and his associates established the Virginia colony in 1584. But the Gulf itself was French; British fishing boats worked the banks outside. Peace between the two nations was partly attributable to a common enemy – Phillip II's Spain, vast, jealous, and implacable in its hatred of Protestants. Until the defeat of the Armada in 1588, the shadows of galleons reached right to Newfoundland.

After Roberval's ill-fated venture, several more official attempts to colonize the Gulf also ended in failure. Then came Samuel de Champlain: soldier, administrator, explorer, cartographer, adventurer, scholar, artist, colonizer.

His first two settlement attempts occurred in the Bay of Fundy. For a time there, in the pastoral arms of the Annapolis Basin in what would later be the heart of Acadia, he took a "particular pleasure" in gardening, an interest which would later expand into large-scale agriculture at Quebec. "Distrust," he mused, gazing out from the stout walls of Port Royal at Basque, English, and Indian raiders, "is the mother of safety."

With Champlain's establishment of Quebec, the centre of commerce shifted westward, away from the Gulf. His later discovery of the Great Lakes drainage basin opened an area of unimagined wealth in furs, and soon afterward the Gulf became primarily a zone of transit, criss-crossed by caravels, surveyed by would-be landlords who fancied this or that bit of coast.

As New France grew, English fear and activity also increased. To the north, Henry Hudson explored the bay that bears his name. To the south, the 1664 purchase of Manhattan gave the British control of the Atlantic seaboard from Florida to Acadia. At the entrance to the Gulf, they reasserted Gilbert's claim to Newfoundland and its inestimable fisheries, and in 1613 the Duke of Argall's destruction of Port Royal underlined the precariousness of the French hold. Cod and furs were everywhere the lure. In 1583 the English chronicler Hakluyt reported a single shipment of furs from Canada to Paris worth one million dollars, and in the same year a typical voyage to the south of the Gulf netted 1,000 per cent.

Despite English challenges and encroachments, the French held on. Tadoussac remained the major seaport, although Matane was used more as settlement grew. Increased navigation made charts necessary, and Champlain provided them, gathering cove-by-cove knowledge from the fishermen and traders who were anchoring each year off new lagoons. His 1612 map presents an approximate configuration of the Gulf and includes the unnamed Magdalens, but there is no sign of Prince Edward Island, and Cape Breton Island is splintered into several pieces, reflecting reports of the Bras d'Or Lakes. Twenty years later, however, Champlain was able to place "Ile St. Jean" (Prince Edward Island) correctly, as well as "Ile de St. Louis" (Miscou), and "Ile Royale" (Cape Breton). Uncertainty about the Magdalens suggested that he himself still had not visited this archipelago and was relying on the descriptions of such old mariners as the one encountered at Canso in 1607, who in that year was on his forty-second voyage to the Gulf.

While the centre of New France grew at Quebec, settlement continued around the Gulf, with sailors immigrating unofficially from scores of small ships. These men knew the Gulf, and they held it tenaciously, cargo by cargo, year after year. Throughout the 1600s, despite British raids and battles won and lost elsewhere, they stayed. Some were beyond reach of all authority, but many found themselves in the service of a *seigneur*, to whom the land on which they lived had been officially granted.

Leasing land *en seigneurie* was a system imported directly from France and used first along the St. Lawrence River. Acreage at Sault au Matelot went to Louis Hebert in 1623, Cap Tourmente to Guillaume de Caen in 1624, and a large tract on the St. Charles River to the Jesuits in 1626, for which they promised to pay with prayers. Secular seigneurs assumed more earthly obligations, including clearing, settling, paying dues, and swearing fealty. A seigneur also took the census, kept records, and submitted reports to Crown agents. In return, the seigneur enjoyed something close to medieval power over his *habitants*; in theory he could dispense corporal punishment and even death. In fact, however, the Canadian seigneurial system was not nearly as onerous as its feudal counterpart, for the habitant was no serf. He was free to move from one seigneury to another, or even to break free temporarily or permanently and follow the beguiling life of a *voyageur* or *coureur de bois*.

Of the seigneuries granted in the Gulf during the seventeenth and eighteenth centuries, three are particularly noteworthy, for they involved almost the entire Gulf of St. Lawrence. The seigneurs were Augustin le Gardeur de Courtemanche, Louis Jolliet, and Nicholas Denys.

Courtemanche's was a vast concession at the top of the Gulf, stretching from Kegashka to Kessessakiou (Hamilton River, Labrador). For ten years from 1702, Courtemanche, a Canadian born at Quebec in 1663, was given a trading and fishing monopoly along this entire coast. He established his headquarters first at the town of Brest in Old Fort Bay, where Jacques Cartier had reprovisioned before

NEAR BERESFORD, NEW BRUNSWICK

SALMON BEACH AREA, NEW BRUNSWICK

his Gulf expedition. Two years later he moved a few kilometres north to "Baie de Phelypeaux," (Bradore), and built a fort called Pontchartrain, after the Minister of Marine.

At Bradore, Courtemanche soon established good relations with the Montagnais, about thirty families of whom lived inside his concession. The Eskimos, however, were a different matter; they were the descendants of the Thule people who had begun to migrate southward about 1350. *Raw-meat eaters*, the Montagnais called them; Inuit, *the people*, they called themselves. Reckless, tough, independent, and jealous of ancestral rights, they waged continuous war against French fishermen, often seizing and burning boats solely for their iron nails. By 1714, Eskimo resentment against white incursions had reached such a point that they descended on Bradore 800 strong. Meeting this threat, Courtemanche used well tested tactics. "All conceivable means must be employed to win over the Eskimos," he had written several years earlier. "These means are: 1) to forbid the French to fire on them; 2) to try to entice or catch a few of them, treat them well in all sorts of ways, and send them back with gifts for themselves and their compatriots; 3) urge a few bold and clever Frenchmen to go among them in order to try to bring them round, or at least to appeal to the Frenchmen who are believed to be among them to persuade them to trade with the French. To this end promise to give good rewards to these Frenchmen ... "

In the spring of 1717, when a group of Eskimos beached near the fort in their wallowing *umiaks*, Courtemanche seized four of them. Three of the captives were women, and one of these, Acoutsina, gave the French community one of the first amicable contacts they appear to have had with the Inuit. Responding to unexpected kindness, Acoutsina learned some French, taught some Inuit, and provided two years of insights into native culture. The French, for example, apparently had not appreciated the depth of the enmity between the Inuit and the Montagnais, whom the Inuit contemptuously called *erpalik*, "lousy." After Courtemanche's death, Acoutsina returned to her people and vanished among them, and the frail link between the cultures was broken. Inuit bellicosity returned and they continued intractable until the advent of Moravian missionaries, fifty years later.

Louis Jolliet and his partner, Jacques de Lalande, had no such problems on their seigneury on the Mingan Islands and Anticosti, although it lay well within Inuit hunting grounds. A restless and inquiring soul, Jolliet had already packed an astonishing amount of scholarship, exploration, and adventure into his thirty-five years before becoming the seigneur of Mingan in 1679. Jesuit training ensured that he knew his history, theology, and classical languages, but he had inclined away from the priesthood and towards business and exploration. By the time he accepted the Mingan grant he was a hero in both Canada and France for his discovery of the Mississippi. Moreover, in pursuing his own and his father-in-law's interests at Sept Iles he had become a considerable merchant, often consulted by Governor Frontenac on matters of policy.

GATHERING IRISH MOSS, NORTH LAKE, PRINCE EDWARD ISLAND

By 1681, Jolliet had established a summer headquarters on Anticosti, moving each year with his family and servants to winter at Quebec. Much of the man's life is shrouded in mystery, partly because he several times lost his papers in fires; but he evidently prospered on the north shore, trading from Mingan to Anticosti and charting the Gulf coasts until 1690. In that year, an Anglo-American fleet under Sir William Phips, on its way to attack Quebec, seized his ship and a fortune in goods. Two years later, the English sacked and burned both his Mingan and Anticosti establishments.

In later years Jolliet's name crops up in various official records; he piloted, he taught, he held government posts. He died in 1700 but we do not know where, nor do we know where he is buried. He may well lie near his old post on the mainland, or on one of the beautiful Mingan islands – as one legend has it, "beside a little lake." On the other hand, the archaeologist René Lévesque, who conducted a careful and unsuccessful search for Jolliet's grave, prefers to believe "que ce grand explorateur est tout simplement disparu lors d'un voyage sur ce fleuve qu'il avait tant parcouru et aime."

It would be good to believe that this is precisely what happened, and that the restlessness of the man merged naturally at last with the eternal movement of water.

One of the earliest and largest seigneuries on the Gulf was granted to Nicholas Denys, who had accompanied the governor, Isaac de Razilly, to Acadia in 1632. Denys's seigneury swept in a great arc around the south end of the Gulf, from Cape Breton to Cap des Rosiers on the Gaspé Peninsula. It included Miscou and Shippegan, Prince Edward Island, and the Magdalens (called, at this time, "Iles Ramées"). He soon established fishing and trading posts at Miscou, at St. Pierre and St. Anne on Cape Breton, and at Nepisiguit (Bathurst, New Brunswick). Denys's life was fraught with betrayals, ambuscades, and imprisonments by commercial rivals. He was destined to live in penury in France during his later years until, bearing the great white beard which had given him his nickname, "La Grande Barbe," he returned to die in a red sandstone house at his beloved Nepisiguit.

He was a fisherman, a lumberman, a speculator, and a seigneur of rare integrity, ebullient optimism, and visionary faith in the coasts he knew well. He was, in fact, probably the foremost figure in the seventeenth-century history of the Gulf.

The site of his post at Miscou remains very close to what it must have been like in 1645. It has the sublime vistas of the Gulf, the soaring sky, and the trim white buildings. To the east, enclosed by slender sandbars that reach towards each other and almost touch, lies a tiny harbour, a perfect shelter. The French named Miscou "Ile de St. Louis," but the Micmac name has prevailed. It means "low, wet, ground," and it has Algonkian offshoots in words such as *muskrat* and *muskeg*. "When one walks upon them," wrote Denys of the Miscou bogs, "they are made to tremble for more than fifty paces around

ST. LUNAIRE BAY, NEAR CAP DEGRAT, NEWFOUNDLAND

LA POINTE, CAPE BRETON ISLAND, NOVA SCOTIA

COD DRYING, CLORIDORME, QUEBEC

him." The little island was a favoured spring and summer resort of the Micmacs, for both seals and walrus lounged by the hundreds on its beaches.

In Micmac legend, Miscou is the home of an androgynous monster.

> ... near Chaleur Bay [wrote Marc Lescarbot, Champlain's historian] lies an isle where lives a dreadful monster called by the savages Gougou, which they told me had a woman's shape, but very terrible, and so tall, said they, that the top of the masts of our vessel would not have reached her waist, so tall do they describe her, and that she has often devoured, and still devours, many savages, whom she puts in a great pouch when she can catch them, and then eats them ... This monster ... makes horrible noises in this island; and when they speak of it, it is always with a strange and unequalled fear ...

More persistently associated with Miscou are rumours of buried treasure. The French gave the name "Ile du Trésor" to a tiny peninsula inside Miscou Harbour, and the English called it "Money Island." However, various digs over the years have turned up little more than gunflints, crockery, silver coins, a pistol, a religious medal, and other normal detritus of settlement or shipwreck.

Other seigneuries were granted during the seventeenth century along the Straits of Canso and Northumberland, but settling them proved difficult. Newcomers found the Gulf shores less attractive than the broad marshlands of Port Royal, Minas, and Beaubassin in the Bay of Fundy. Properly diked, those grasslands made rich farms, although the process of draining them and cleansing them of salt took several years. A 1686 census showed 583 people living at Port Royal, fifty-seven at Minas, and 127 at Beaubassin, while there were only two or three homesteading families at Nepisiguit and Miramichi on the shores of the Gulf.

Percé, on the Gaspé Peninsula, was much more attractive. The same census named five families totalling twenty-six people living there in 1686, and this population was swollen annually by the seasonal arrival of the cod fleets. In August 1690, two Anglo-American corsairs moved partly by anti-Catholic zeal and partly by the yen for booty, sacked all habitations at Percé and Bonaventure, "despoyling great quantitys of fish ... They remained there for eight entire days," wrote Father Emmanuel Jumeau to his superior, "during which they committed a hundred impieties, with all the excesses imaginable." Only one month later the little settlement was again ravaged, this time by Phips's squadron on its way to attack Quebec.

Vulnerable to such piracy and depredation, the Gaspé settlements were not repeopled for

SERPENTINE TABLELAND, LONG RANGE MOUNTAINS NEAR TROUT RIVER, NEWFOUNDLAND

several years after that last assault. In 1711, Sir Hovendon Walker found only one French ship to burn in Gaspé Bay. When settlements were re-established on the peninsula, they appeared at the traditional five places: Matane, the farthest point upriver where cod might be caught; Mount Louis, where Denis Riverin had briefly established a little colony in 1699; Gaspé Bay, the magnificent and traditional sheltering-place for ships of all nations; Ile Percée and Baie des Morues, where the richness of the fishery compensated for the scarcity of good drying beaches; and, finally, Pabos and Grande Rivière, where alluvial deposits had formed protective *barachoises* behind which shallow-draft fishing boats, *chaloupes*, found calm anchorage.

Halfway between the two major French colonies of Canada and Acadia, Gaspé's position was always strategic, its ownership disputed. Resident Micmacs even now claim the Peninsula, insisting that they have never signed a treaty with either French or British. Whatever the legal validity of their claim, they have in fact been dispossessed by the indifference of their ancestors and the cunning of white administrators. Hunting freely through the interior, many generations of Micmacs in the first years of contact must have scoffed at the white coast-dwellers' obsession with cod, only to realize too late that these interlopers had come to stay and to claim. Gradually their ancestral seaboard was diminished to the mouths of the Miramichi and the Restigouche, where their myths said that God had created man and given him Gaspé. By 1623, when Father Gabriel Sagard arrived to do battle with "Satan and his imps," the territorial battle, never really fought by the Micmacs, had already been lost.

However, many other battles occurred among the newcomers themselves. The first major naval engagement in the Gulf was fought off Gaspé in the spring of 1628, when a Quebec-bound French fleet loaded with colonists and supplies met a squadron commanded by the English privateer David Kirke, fresh from ravaging Miscou. The French surrendered after an exchange of several hours, leaving Quebec open to English seizure the following year.

Easily distinguished by its jutting headlands and lacking proper defences, Gaspé was frequently a battleground during almost a century and a half of hostilities. All settlements there were vulnerable to sweeps from privateers, *les forbans*, and from British frigates. In a restless and renegade country the exposed extremities of Gaspé were particularly lawless. Yet, despite all adversity, the Gaspésiens endured. They caught and dried their cod and they held onto their beaches. With a resilience and independence that characterizes their descendants to this day, they enforced their own laws on their own frontier. They and other settlers on the shore quietly and persistently kept the Gulf French.

Settlements do not become communities until women live in them and until families take root and grow. Whether they were Indian girls taken *à la fashion du pays*, or *filles du roi*, or wives who had immigrated with their husbands, the first Canadian women were stabilizers and consolidators; their task was nothing

ST. GEORGE'S BAY, NEAR STEPHENVILLE, NEWFOUNDLAND

less than the domestication of the land, and that was a far more daunting challenge than most had faced in France.

Their first task was usually to help build some type of shelter. Often these were simply *piquets*, rough shacks braced with poles and not intended to last more than one season. Later, more ambitious house-builders sometimes worked under civil restrictions (a 1721 ordinance at Louisbourg, for example, limited the height of houses so they would not interfere with the cod-drying winds), but usually they were limited only by funds, energy, imagination, and convention. The common type of small house with steep roof, flared eaves, and small windows made obvious sense in cold climates, and was brought from the Isle and Dordogne valleys. Short of wood since the Middle Ages, Europeans used as much masonry as possible, but construction in New France relied on the abundant forests. Not only were the roofs wooden, but frequently the walls were as well; and if they were not all wood they were at least *colombage*, half-timbered, a mixture of squared logs and masonry. The preferred form in all-log houses was *pièce-sur-pièce*, in which short logs were tenoned into upright posts placed at regular intervals. In some cases, dovetailing was used, but this method seems to have emerged later under English influence. Heavy shutters could be swung across the ground-floor windows, to keep out both cold and intruders, and fireplaces at both ends of the house were preferred. The attic, where children and servants slept, may or may not have been lighted and ventilated by small dormers in the end walls.

A settler's life fell quickly into patterns determined by the season and the sea. The period from spring breakup until midsummer was the time for catching cod and making fish. From midsummer until late October, attention turned to the catching of herring, and then the weirs would stretch out spindly arms to gather their prey. Eels, lobsters, and molluscs were taken anytime.

October was the month for gathering the winter's supply of wood. Along the north shore, this involved considerable expenditure of time and energy, as year by year the desirable dried and twisted roots of low-blown spruce were used up from areas close to the settlement. On early trips, stacks of these roots were cut and piled. After the first snows they were tied onto *komatiks*, flat Eskimo sledges, and hauled by dogs back to the settlement. From November to March, the habitants turned to hunting and trapping, with fox, mink, muskrat, lynx, and beaver being the major game. In late March and April, as the ice began to break up and the great annual migration of the harp seals began, dwellers along the coasts moved outward for the harvesting of these animals.

In agricultural regions, life fell into similar rhythms. From June to September, the colonist had to make best use of good weather for seeding, haymaking, and harvesting. In Catholic New France, however, eighty or ninety of these potential working days were lost to various religious observances, although community *corvées*, or bees, likely more than compensated for the time taken by the Church.

ST. JOHN ISLAND, NEWFOUNDLAND

ABOVE: ICEBERG, FORTEAU BAY, LABRADOR, NEWFOUNDLAND

OPPOSITE: NEAR OLD FORT, QUEBEC

People gathered together for corn-shuckings, flax-beatings, barn-raisings, and other co-operative activities, and these would be followed by evening celebrations at which the fiddlers playing brisk jigs and quadrilles were central figures.

A French officer, recording impressions of Canada in 1755, said that Canadians seemed ant-like in their activities: "They provide themselves with everything for the winter while summer is still with us ... They stock up with meat as if they would eat it at a single meal, and they put it in a storehouse where it freezes and is thus preserved ... "

Smoking and salting were the other common ways of preserving all meat. Corn, oats, barley, peas, lentils, beans, and asparagus were preferred vegetables from the beginning of settlement, with cabbages, celery, shallots, onions, carrots, and pumpkins coming into favour later on. Early settlers abhorred potatoes – "never intended to be used as food for human beings," one writer said – but they loved maize and used it in a variety of ways. Women around the Gulf also cultivated a little fruit where possible, and gathered wild berries in season – strawberries, raspberries, wild plums, blackberries, cranberries, currants, wild cherries, and bilberries.

One of the commonest farmers' dishes was the *pièce tourtière*, a kind of meat-and-vegetable pie into which went whatever was available, stewed and seasoned. On the coast, the equivalent of the tourtière was a casserole called the *sipaille* (from the English "sea-pie"), containing a variety of fishes, herbs, and vegetables. Such dishes were supplemented with large quantities of bread; the average hard-working farmer or fisherman usually ate two pounds of bread in four meals a day. Because they were aware of the caloric requirements of such men, Church officials often turned a blind eye to dietary violations during Lent or on Fridays; or else they invented circumventions, such as allowing the consumption of beaver and muskrat because these animals were amphibious and, therefore, half fish. Vast quantities of milk were drunk with meals, as well as cider, spruce beer, and *cerevisia*, a fermented brew made from barley. Wines and liquors were usually kept for special occasions. Beech nuts, honey, maple syrup, and cakes made up dessert.

Substantial food and lots of it made for a healthy and vigorous people. Despite the cold and the hardships, there is little doubt that the common settler on the shores of the Gulf was better off than his counterpart in France. Travellers noted that he was larger and more robust. In fact, he was probably better fed than the average twentieth-century North American.

The wealth of Canada guaranteed that the Gulf would be drawn into European conflicts. The years following Cartier's voyages and Champlain's colonization were strewn with claims and counterclaims, truces and treaties, but despite all English challenges, the seventeenth century closed with the French

OLD HARRY AREA, MAGDALEN ISLANDS, QUEBEC

NEAR L'ANSE PLEUREUSE, GASPÉ PENINSULA, QUEBEC

NEAR WESTERN BROOK POND, GREAT NORTHERN PENINSULA, NEWFOUNDLAND

firmly in possession of the Gulf. The early 1700s were troubled years in the new land as in Europe, made more harrowing in the Gulf by the raids of Indians. A series of French governors had waged war against the Iroquois, who had become English shock troops, and British fishermen in the Gulf were so terrified of the Micmacs that even in times of open war they liked to have a French vessel close at hand.

By 1700, the British had not managed even to acquire accurate charts of the Gulf. In 1690, when Sir William Phips left Boston to attack Quebec, his thirty-two ships and 2,000 men were sailing blind as they entered the mouth of the river. No French pilot would guide them, and Phips's groping journeys up the river and back again were more harrowing than his attack on the Citadel itself. In disarray, Phips's squadron straggled back down the St. Lawrence, leaving wrecked ships as it went. Part of the crew of one brigantine wintered on Anticosti and was miraculously saved by another Boston ship in the spring.

The Treaty of Ryswick in 1697 left the Gulf French, but the wounds of the long conflict had scarcely closed before the War of the Spanish Succession (Queen Anne's War) brought fresh eruptions in 1701. This time, British depredations around the Gulf were more severe, and the threat to Quebec itself was more serious. New England greatly feared the growing French presence curving behind it down the Mississippi, closing off all expansion to the west. As well, Boston and New York merchants envied the wealth of New France. Now was the time to strike, when French naval power in America was weaker than it had been for many years.

In the summer of 1711, an assault force of 12,000 marines and seasoned British regulars put to sea, bound for Quebec. They were borne in sixty transports and escorted by nine ships of the line as well as various bomb vessels and tenders. Larger than the entire population of Boston, this force had been mustered in utmost secrecy, and word of Quebec's peril did not reach the Citadel until the fleet was already in the Gulf.

From the quarterdeck of the flagship *Edgar* on the evening of 22 August, the admiral of this fleet examined the north coast of the Gulf. The curving shore of the Gaspé Peninsula had been bleak enough, with its isolated clusters of houses and fishing sheds, but this north shore was utterly barren and desolate, a godforsaken place. The admiral was happy to bring the fleet about to the southwest, into open water.

Sir Hovenden Walker was neither a brilliant leader nor a navigator. Eighteenth-century patronage being what it was, he probably owed his command less to ability than to Tory friendships. Nevertheless, he was no fool. Before leaving Boston he had been disturbed by reading Phips's harrowing account of navigation on the St. Lawrence, and by discovering that there were still no reliable charts. He had given the job of guiding the fleet to Colonel Samuel Vetch, who commanded the colonial irregulars and who knew the Gulf and river well from years of contraband trade with the French. However, as they rounded

ABOVE: BUCTOUCHE AREA, NEW BRUNSWICK

OPPOSITE: BRADORE BAY, QUEBEC

Gaspé, Vetch inexplicably refused to act as pilot and Walker accepted his refusal. Hastily, he commandeered the captain of a French ship, one Jean Paradis, to take the fleet up the river to Quebec. Paradis, a small-time smuggler who had already had one ship clawed out from under him on the Manicougan reefs, agreed. Whether he did so from avidity or guile we shall never know. He was dead within fifteen years, taking his secret with him. Vetch, however, warned against him, describing him as "an ignorant, pretending, idle, drunken Fellow."

Walker's trepidation mounted when the fleet encountered fog near Anticosti. Coming just as they were entering the river, it must have seemed like the worst of omens. Fearing to risk his largest ships, Walker split the squadron, leaving four cruisers and the *Humber* and *Devonshire*, each of eighty guns, to patrol the Gulf in his rear.

On the evening of 22 August, west of Anticosti, he issued his last order and retired for the night. He believed he was safely in mid-channel on a port tack towards the south shore. What he did not know was that the strong and capricious currents of the St. Lawrence had been at work, and that the *Edgar* and the fleet were actually heading directly for the Pointe des Monts promontory of the north shore.

Shortly after he had retired, Walker was awakened by the watch, who had spied land ahead through the breaking fog. Walker did not go on deck; he assumed that they were nearing the Gaspé coast and, therefore, he gave an order to wear and come about to starboard. In the circumstances this was a fatal command which sent the great ships bearing down on the reefs of Egg Island. Bringing an eighteenth-century square-rigger about through the eye of the wind required at least ten minutes even if all the crew were at their stations. For Walker's fleet, time ran out.

By the time the alarm was sounded and the admiral had reached his quarterdeck, some transports were already on the reefs. Distress flares and ghastly moonlight shone on destruction. Only fast action and a providential shift in the wind prevented the loss of the entire squadron. As it was, seven transports and one storeship smashed into pieces and nearly 900 people died; 150 sailors, 700 soldiers, and thirty-five women.

For two days Walker cruised offshore searching for survivors. Badly shaken, he then held a council of war with his senior officers, abandoned the expedition to Quebec, and stood back out into the Gulf. The disaster would haunt him all his life, and his efforts to exonerate himself would be made no easier by the loss of his journals and log in the explosion of the *Edgar* shortly after her arrival in England.

News of the English fleet's destruction reached Quebec in a strange manner. On 13 August, a young French officer stationed at Fort Pontchartrain in Bradore Bay received an urgent order from the

Ministry of Marine to alert Quebec to an imminent English attack; the object of the expedition had been tardily discovered by French spies.

The officer's name was François Margane de Lavaltrie; he was twenty-six. Immediately, he set out with a picked crew of paddlers for Quebec, over 1,200 kilometres away. The journey along the north shore took him almost a month, and he must have passed very close to the vanguard of Walker's fleet, perhaps in darkness, perhaps in fog. In fact, had his departure been only slightly delayed, he would have discovered the calamity while it was still fresh, with English men-o'-war hovering offshore.

At Quebec he delivered his warning, left on 18 September, and headed back down the coast, expecting to pass the English on his way. Thirteen days out, inside Egg Island, he came upon the site of Walker's catastrophe. First he saw the wreckage, broken masts and shredded canvas; then the flotsam and jetsam, strewn thick above the tide-line; and then, the dozens of corpses, bloating on the long crescent of shore. The British had left no burial party. Scavengers were already at work.

Lavaltrie returned to Quebec with the news, and the city celebrated with the pealing of church bells. It was spring before an official salvage expedition left the city, and by then much had fallen into the hands of scavengers. What was left was auctioned. For years, skulls and bones littered the shore.

In England, Walker kissed the hand of Queen Anne. "I said, I was very sorry my Power to serve Her Majesty in the late Expedition, had not been equal to my Zeal ... " As for Lavaltrie, the young adventurer who had brought the good news to Quebec, he was given the fertile mouth of the St. Augustin River as a seigneury in 1720, and conducted a trading and fishing business there for seventeen years before leasing his concession and following his wife into holy orders. He died peacefully at Quebec on 6 March 1750, a priest.

Two years after the Walker expedition, Queen Anne's War ended with the Treaty of Utrecht, a disastrous compromise for the French of the Gulf. Under its terms they lost all of Acadia (roughly, the three maritime provinces, the north coast of Maine, the southern coast of the Gaspé Peninsula, and the Magdalen Islands), and almost all of Newfoundland, retaining only the right to catch and cure fish around the tip of the northern peninsula. With that treaty the long struggle of the Acadians began, for they refused to leave the farms they had so laboriously drained and diked, and they refused also to acknowledge the sovereignty of the British monarch. Finally they would embarrass the British in the eyes of history, by forcing the clearance and dispersion of 1755.

At the southern entry to the Gulf, the French kept control of Cape Breton Island. Here, in an ice-free bay on the east coast, deep enough to receive the doughtiest corsairs and with enough good beaches to satisfy cod fishermen, they began construction of Louisbourg in 1720.

OVERLEAF, LEFT: MABOU AREA, CAPE BRETON ISLAND, NOVA SCOTIA
OVERLEAF, RIGHT: GRANDE ENTRÉE, MAGDALEN ISLANDS, QUEBEC

Louisbourg was a doomed and foggy fortress. In its scandalous twenty years of construction, Louisbourg so drained the imperial treasury that Louis XV declared he expected to see its towers from Versailles. In its heyday the fortress was a bustling entrepôt where goods were exchanged from all points, and where a lively contraband trade was carried on with the American colonists to the south. Such trade rankled official New England, still apprehensive of the French arm circling from Canada down the Mississippi and into Louisiana. "There is no repose for our thirteen colonies," wrote Ben Franklin, "so long as the French are masters of Canada."

Consequently, when the War of the Austrian Succession (King George's War) broke out in 1743, and when raiders from Louisbourg seized a British fishing station at Canso, the New Englanders assembled a force of 4,200 volunteers and struck at the fortress itself. According to their commodore they were "the greatest set of cowards and poltroons ... all bluster, noise ...," but in six weeks they had captured Louisbourg and its mutinous garrison. "The General went in and took Possession of the Citty of Louisbourg!" wrote one Massachusetts militiaman. "The greatest Conquest, that Ever was Gain'd by New England."

The victory atoned for a humiliating defeat in 1707, when the colonial troops managed to kill only a few cows in an attack on Port Royal, and returned to Boston to be met by jeering women brandishing wooden swords and shouting, "Is yor piss-pot charg'd, neighbour? So-ho, souse ye cowards! Salute Port Royal!" The victory also encouraged later resistance against the British in the American Revolution.

From Louisbourg the Americans launched an expedition into the Gulf and attacked Prince Edward Island, burning the communities at Three Rivers and Port Lajoie. One spirited French captain named Duvivier withdrew up the Hillsborough River, gathered his forces, and counter-attacked with sufficient strength to repel the raiders. But the respite was temporary, and until the end of the war French settlers on the island lived under the shadow of deportation, part of the British plan to "extirpate the French from North America." Only the lack of transports prevented the accomplishment of this aim.

To the disgust of New England, the Treaty of Aix-la-Chapelle in 1748 restored both Cape Breton and Prince Edward Island to the French, and the fleur-de-lis once again flew over Louisbourg. Lower Nova Scotia and Acadia remained under British rule, however, and the dogged struggle of the Acadians neared its climax.

Proud and stubborn, the Acadians were rooted to their soil. They were the first Canadians. For them, home was not somewhere else; home was here, and here they would stay. The heart of Acadia lay at the head of the Bay of Fundy, in Chignecto Bay and Cobequid Bay, particularly the area of the brooding Tantramar Marshes, hundreds of acres of which the Acadians had patiently drained, diked, and reclaimed.

As the British advanced from the south, some settlers crossed the Isthmus of Chignecto, bound for the French coasts of New Brunswick and Nova Scotia. In 1730, the population of Prince Edward Island was 325; by 1752 that number had grown to 2,223, and by 1758 to about 4,500. Acadian farms were spread throughout the island from Malpeque to Souris, with the heaviest concentrations in the Prim Peninsula, around Hillsborough Bay, and up the Hillsborough valley to St. Peter's Bay. At the same time, Acadian settlements grew elsewhere in the Gulf – at Miramichi, Chaleur, and Cheticamp on Cape Breton.

Stimulating both migration and guerrilla action against the British was Jean-Louis Le Loutre, Vicar-General of the Bishop of Quebec and head of the clergy in Acadia. Le Loutre was an intense, restless, proselytizing activist who remained zealously opposed to any accommodation with the enemy. Very early the British had placed a price on his head. In 1750 Le Loutre urged a scorched-earth policy ahead of a force of redcoats advancing up the Bay of Fundy. Many Acadians responded and moved north to resettle in the Tantramar, where the French constructed a new fort, Beauséjour, within sight of the British Fort Lawrence.

Fort Lawrence had been particularly threatening to the French, because of the strategic importance of the Isthmus of Chignecto. This narrow neck of land had traditionally been the portage and communication route between Canada and Acadia, through the Baie Verte settlement. More importantly, the boundaries of Acadia had not been precisely defined under the Treaty of Utrecht. All of New Brunswick was in dispute, and if the British could assert their claim, through Chignecto, to the Gulf Coast of New Brunswick, they would break French control of the Gulf. Chignecto was therefore crucial, and the French sought to protect it with Beauséjour on the south side, Fort Gaspereau on the Gulf side, and a string of outposts between. The tiny Missaguash River had become an unofficial boundary, and during the undeclared war from 1750 to 1755 it remained so.

Both English and French paid for scalps, and there were shameful incidents such as the one in 1750 – when an English officer well known to the garrison at Beauséjour was shot down under a flag of truce. In general, however, relations between the adjacent garrisons at Forts Beauséjour and Lawrence were more wary than hostile; considerable fraternization took place, and local Acadian farmers freely sold produce to both garrisons.

Beneath the surface the area was seething with intrigue and venality. In 1754 the commandant at Beauséjour, Louis Du Pont Duchambon de Vergor (described by one lady as "the most dull-witted fellow I have ever met ... "), received the following encouragement to graft from the Intendant of New France, François Bigot: "Profit, my dear Vergor, by your position; trim, cut – you have the power – do

OVERLEAF: RED BAY, LABRADOR, NEWFOUNDLAND

it quickly so that you may be able to come and join me in France and purchase an estate near mine." The Intendant's letter provides a rueful insight into the state of administration in Acadia and Canada during the last French years. Even Montcalm was not immune to influence, for despite his repeated claims that Canada was making him poor it was discovered, after his death, that with Bigot's help he had amassed a fortune.

At Beauséjour throughout the years before its fall, Le Loutre schemed and laboured for a British defeat. One of his serious errors, however, was in recommending a minor functionary named Thomas Pichon to an official post within the fort, for shortly after his appointment the English enlisted Pichon as a spy. "He gave me to understand," said Pichon of Captain George Scott, commandant at Fort Lawrence, "that he knew of means which were very safe, and that I should have no cause for regret, if I accepted his proposal." While resident at Beauséjour, Pichon spied constantly for the English. "We established a correspondence," he said, "which was most active."

One of the items that passed between them was the news that Vergor had received orders from Quebec to attack Fort Lawrence. This intelligence made little difference to the English, however, because they had already laid plans to attack Beauséjour; and they did so on 2 June 1755, with a force of 300 regulars and 2,000 Massachusetts volunteers. Within two weeks the fort fell. Two days afterwards, the French surrendered Gaspereau without a shot.

With these defeats, the fate of the Acadians was sealed. For the final time, their representatives refused to take the British oath of allegiance. They were cleared from their lands by force, many taking with them vials of the earth they loved, and within a few years English-speaking colonists had replaced them throughout Nova Scotia.

The hapless Vergor would make only one more appearance in Canadian history. At Quebec he was in command of the outpost above the Foulon when Wolfe's troops landed. Not only were his sentries negligent but Vergor, still profiting from his position, is said to have weakened his guard by letting militiamen return home for the harvest – on condition that they do some work on his farm as well.

The spring that Beauséjour fell, a large French fleet with most of its guns *en flute* (unmounted, to accommodate soldiers on the decks), carrying the new governor to Canada, was intercepted in the Gulf by Admiral Edward "Wry-necked Dick" Boscawen. Fog allowed most of the French ships to escape upriver to Quebec, but despite typhoid among his crews Boscawen took two prizes.

War had not yet been declared, but the days of French sovereignty in Canada were numbered. The English net was tightening. British men-o'-war patrolled the Gulf with impunity, outnumbering the

French two-to-one. The grand design of encircling the English with a French scimitar from the Gulf through the Great Lakes and down the Mississippi to Louisiana was about to crumble forever. The decisive blows would fall on either side of the Gulf of St. Lawrence, first at Louisbourg and then at Quebec, and the same man would help deliver both.

Brigadier-General James Wolfe was thirty-one in 1758. The son of an officer, he had entered military service early, and had seen his first action in Holland when he was sixteen. He was a slight man with a receding chin and an unfortunate, triangular profile that was a satirist's delight. However, he compensated for his ill looks, his poor health, and his intellectual limitations with ambition, a rigour that bordered on asceticism, and a scrupulous concern for detail and for the welfare of his men. He was a dedicated soldier with a stern code of personal morality and professional ethics – a rare type in the politico-military hierarchy of his time.

That sternness sometimes manifested itself in harshness towards enemies. He was present when Cumberland's troops massacred the Scottish clans at Culloden; and after the fall of Louisbourg he spread devastation through the Gulf, directed principally against the civilian population. Later, piqued that his first attacks on Quebec had been repelled, he razed St. Lawrence farms and habitations. "I found that good Treatment had not the deemed Effect," he wrote to Pitt, "so that of late I have changed my Measures & laid waste the country ... " This destruction continued for two months until some of his own officers protested.

The men, however, regarded him with affection and respect. He was feverishly energetic and flamboyantly reckless. A few years earlier he had written in a premonitory letter to his mother, " ... as I rise in rank people will expect some considerable performances, and I shall be induced, in support of an ill-got reputation, to be lavish of my life and shall probably meet the fate which is the ordinary effect of such conduct."

On 29 May 1758, 16,000 troops under the command of Major-General Jeffery Amherst sailed from Halifax to attack Louisbourg. The fleet of 150 ships was commanded by Edward Boscawen. James Wolfe was one of three brigade commanders.

Amherst had no illusions about his task. Louisbourg was indeed formidable, but in 1754 the spy Pichon had reported: "The curtain [i.e. wall] between the Queen's bastion and the Princess demi-bastion is dilapidated. The right face of the latter is somewhat impaired and the demi-flank which looks towards the sea is in such bad shape that it would collapse with the first discharge of a cannon on the top, or if a shot were fired at it." Amherst also knew, however, that the French had been labouring hard to shore up the fortifications, and that artillery waited to prevent the British from landing in Gabarus Bay as they had done in 1745.

NEAR SAVAGE HARBOUR, PRINCE EDWARD ISLAND

CAP AU RENARD AREA, GASPÉ PENINSULA, QUEBEC

Good luck was with him. Part of Wolfe's party, led by George Scott, ex-commander of Fort Lawrence, veered right against orders and found shelter from French fire behind a low ridge in L'Anse de la Cormorandière. From here they were able to gain the heights and to sweep the defenders off the shore and back into the fortress. Wolfe had been placed in charge of a unit of picked troops which he led so effectively – "a mortar in one pocket and a 24-pounder in the other" – in Indian-style hit-and-run, that they gradually took the perimeter and laid seige to the entire north side of the fortress. Entrenched, Wolfe then moved up artillery within range both of the walls and of the four warships that were supposed to have defended Louisbourg harbour. Only one vessel escaped the fall of the fortress. The *Arethuse*, commanded by Jean Vauquelin, withstood the British bombardment until the end, and then ran Boscawen's blockade and escaped to France, battered but with colours high.

Wolfe's energy and success inspired others. "I was in the trenches by daylight this morning," William Amherst recorded on 25 July. "Br. Wolfe was in a great hurry to have the scaling ladders ready; desired me to speak about them to the General. We have pushed on a boyau [trench] within 50 yards of the glacis [outermost parapet]; very smart fire from the covered way on the workmen, which did us very little hurt. Sailors employed last night in drawing the cannon to Br. Wolfe's new battery ... Scaling ladders were sent to the trenches this evening."

By 25 July, short of food and supplies, surrounded by rubble and ringed by the muzzles of the British fleet, Drucour, the governor of Louisbourg, faced the choice of agreeing to terms or seeing the fortress stormed with no quarter. The garrison laid down their arms. They had delayed the British attack on Quebec for one year, but now the Gulf lay open.

The British pushed their advantage. By September, Boscawen and Wolfe were ravaging the Gulf with six ships of the line, six transports full of troops, and assorted other vessels. Wolfe established his headquarters on the Penouille in Gaspé Bay, and from there he directed the destruction of other ports on the Gaspé Peninsula and the deportation of the inhabitants. In Gaspé Bay alone his men destroyed over 30,000 kilograms of fish destined for Quebec.

Other British forces were busy elsewhere in the Gulf. Troops under Colonel James Murray descended on the Acadian refugees at Miramichi and rounded up most, although some escaped with their leader, Boishébert, to carry on guerrilla warfare. The name *Burnt Church* commemorates, to this day, one of the English depredations. Later, in 1758, Lord Rollo was sent from Louisbourg with four ships and 500 troops to clear the French from Prince Edward Island, which had become a huge Acadian refugee camp. He did his job efficiently, packing between 2,000 and 3,000 people into nine transports for deportation to Europe. Seven hundred perished when the *Duke William* and the *Violet*, two of the larger

PUFFIN, ST. MARY'S ISLAND, QUEBEC

ships, sank in transit. Refugees who fled to the western end of the island were taken away by friendly schooners to the Magdalens, to St. Pierre and Miquelon, and to the mainland. "The treatment of the English," wrote de Villejouin, the last French governor of Prince Edward Island, "does not make one wish to be under their rule ... " By 1763, of the 4,700 French who had once inhabited the island, only 300 remained.

"We have done a great deal of mischief," Wolfe wrote as he headed home to England, " ... spread the terror of His Majesty's arms through the whole Gulf; but have added nothing to the reputation of them." Ill "both with the gravel & Rheumatism," Wolfe was promoted to major-general. To a politician who protested and called Wolfe mad, George II is said to have replied, "Mad is he? Then I hope he will bite some of my other generals!"

The second of the crucial battles for Canada was fought after a long siege the next year, beneath the walls of Quebec. It was made possible by the bold seamanship of Admiral Charles Saunders who, with good pilots and the painstaking charts made the previous year by James Cook, brought the British fleet of forty-nine warships and 119 troop transports safely through the Gulf and up the estuary that had defeated Phips and Walker. The French had removed all navigational aids, but not even the tricky Traverse below Ile d'Orléans, where the currents of the forked river rejoin and meet the highest tides in the estuary, presented problems for Cook and the other pilots. Cook had not erred when he announced that June that he was "satisfied with being acquainted with ye channel."

After a restless and unprofitable summer, before dawn on 13 September 1759, a force under Wolfe's command slipped past French sentries and landed at L'Anse au Foulon, at the western end of the Plains of Abraham. Their landing was a final bit of seamanship by Admiral Charles Holmes – "The most hazardous and difficult Task I was ever engaged in." Wolfe's troops quickly overpowered Vergor's picket and for four hours British regiments climbed the slopes and marshalled on the Plains of Abraham. Montcalm rose after a troubled night to see ranks of red coats beyond the slate roofs and mists of Quebec. "C'est serieux!" he said.

Wolfe had taken a last desperate chance before the winter. Several earlier probes against the city had failed. He and many of his troops were ill and, despite their discipline, would surely have been crushed had Montcalm waited for Bougainville's regiments, resting within a short march of the city. But Montcalm did not wait. Concerned lest the British entrench, he ordered an attack and, even before the ranks were properly dressed, allowed them to surge forward. As they advanced their formation broke down further, and their fire grew more scattered and ineffective.

When the French front rank was only thirty-five paces away, the redcoats rose from the grass and fired once, each Brown Bess musket charged with two three-quarter inch balls. More scattered volleys followed – and then the terrible British bayonet charge, Highland claymores whirling at the front. So quick was the French retreat to the city that not a single battle-flag was captured. Wolfe died on the battlefield, shot through the lungs; Montcalm died the following morning. Many of the Canadian troops simply dropped their arms and went home for the harvest. Their Indian allies faded like shadows. As for the surviving French regulars, many escaped to Montreal where there was, throughout that last winter, a baleful atmosphere of abandonment and frivolity as the British pincers tightened.

*T*he coup de grâce to the French regime was struck at the mouth of the Restigouche River. Ironically, it was here in Chaleur Bay that Cartier had made his first exchanges with the Indians 230 years earlier.

In May of 1760, a French fleet intended for the relief of Quebec took shelter. It had suffered a vexed crossing. Just three ships remained from the original fleet; the other three had been lost to Boscawen's blockade and to weather. In the middle of the Gulf, near Ile aux Oiseaux, the French had seized a small British ship on its way to Quebec, and thus learned that a reinforcing English fleet had preceded them upriver and would beat them to Quebec.

This was the worst possible news for troops and seamen already depressed by enemy victories and uncertain of their fate. Their commander, François-Chenard Giraudais, had orders to go to Louisiana should the British win the race to Quebec, and so he probably intended only to rest briefly and take on water at Restigouche, where there was still a sizable pocket of Acadian refugees and guerrillas. He proceeded to Chaleur Bay and led his little squadron among the shoals and shallows deep into the estuary of the Restigouche. Of the three vessels only one, the frigate *Machault*, was a warship; the other two were armed merchantmen.

The British knew of their arrival, and two intercepting squadrons were dispatched from separate ports. The *Prince of Orange*, the *Rochester*, and the *Eurus* proceeded immediately down from Quebec with orders to search the lower St. Lawrence and "the Gulph," while the *Fame*, the *Achilles*, the *Dorsetshire*, the *Scarborough*, and the *Repulse*, under the command of John "Foul Weather Jack" Byron, grandfather of the poet, were sent from Louisbourg. Acting on a hunch, Byron ordered his ships to rendezvous off Miguasha Point at the entrance to Restigouche Harbour. When they had all arrived, he went in.

The battle began on 24 June, when English sailors taking soundings were chased by French boats. Until 2 July, the English groped chartless into the bay, harassed by French and Micmac muskets along the banks. Finally, a land party drove the snipers from a major emplacement and struck into the Acadian refugee community, burning 150 or 200 buildings. From that point French fortunes fell until, after a sharp engagement on 8 July, Giraudais scuttled the *Machault* and the *Bienfaisant*. He would no

ABOVE: MANITOU RIVER, QUEBEC

OPPOSITE: NEAR CAP DES ROSIERS, GASPÉ PENINSULA, QUEBEC

doubt have sent the *Marquis de Malauze* to the bottom as well had she not contained English prisoners; he knew they would have been slaughtered by frenzied Micmacs had they been taken ashore. Later, when the prisoners had been saved, this ship was blown up by the English with the loss of six of the boarding party who could not leave her casks of wine soon enough.

The English then proceeded systematically to sink all other vessels in the bay – twenty-two or twenty-three Acadian chaloupes. Then, on the evening of 8 July, Byron's squadron broke off and swung downstream towards the Gulf, leaving destruction amidst the shoals behind. Off Pointe à la Batterie they paused for an issue of rum.

Later that year, Montreal surrendered and New France fell. Only pockets of resistance remained. One held out at Restigouche until two more British expeditions had silenced it for good. Another, consisting of thirteen marines, fought for some time around the mouth of the Miramichi. By 1761, however, the Gulf was firmly British, the French retaining only tenuous fishing rights around the northern tip of Newfoundland, as well as the ports of St. Pierre and Miquelon to service cod fleets from the Grand Banks.

For the *Canadiens* living around the Gulf, the conquest was not complete disaster. Although they did not relish living under British rule, the end of hostilities meant also the end of obligatory militia service and the beginning of the end of Anglo-American harassment. Most important, the Gulf was too big and its population too scattered to be threatened with anything similar to the Acadian deportations of five years earlier; it was, after all, impossible to deport a nation of 65,000 people. So, boats could be built and sailed again, fish caught, life lived.

As for the British, they began at once to measure and assess what they had won. In fact, the process began before the conquest was complete. Coasts had to be charted, channels sounded, and harbours mapped. All such practical surveying matters were attended to by military engineers, and their job was immense. Even where charting and buoying had already been done, the French had destroyed all navigational aids lest they assist the invaders.

On the day after Louisbourg fell, an ordnance engineer named Samuel Jan Holland was at work on a beach near the fortress. Offshore lay the *Pembroke*, a warship of sixty guns that had been engaged throughout the battle. Holland had a meeting with a young officer from that ship: " ... I observed Capt. Cook particularly attentive to my operations; and as he expressed an ardent desire to be instructed in the use of the Plane Table (the instrument I was then using) I appointed the next day in order to make him acquainted with the whole process ... "

James Cook was then thirty and at a turning point in his career. He had served a hard apprenticeship in coal ships along England's treacherous east coast, had volunteered for the navy, and had risen rapidly to his position as master of the *Pembroke.* As master, his duties under the captain included navigation, sounding, charting, and keeping the log. These were duties that Cook had cheerfully accepted.

His curiosity about Holland's plane table (a device for measuring angles), led him to study trigonometry, geometry, and astronomy under Holland's guidance, and in the succeeding months the two of them made the first comprehensive British survey of the Gulf. Cook kept copious notes. "Cape Gaspey," he wrote in his graceful script, "is very remarkable the NE side being high steep white clifts, and close by it stands a white rock called the Old Women when this rock is open of the Cape and you are some distance off it appears like a sail."

In January 1761, Cook was awarded fifty pounds "in consideration of his indefatigable Industry in making himself Master of the pilotage of the River Saint Lawrence, &c." In 1763 the Admiralty ordered him to make charts of Newfoundland. This endeavour would occupy him for five years, until he sailed for the Pacific.

Meantime, other surveyors were also busy in the Gulf. Holland was appointed Surveyor-General of Canada in 1764, and he in turn appointed a deputy and several assistants, among them Peter Haldimand, a young officer "of no vices but expensive tastes," who had served throughout the Seven Years' War and conducted several surveys afterwards. Haldimand was sent first to Prince Edward Island, renowned for its fertility, in order to parcel it out for British settlement. He found there about thirty families of Acadians who had escaped deportation. They were reduced to a subsistence level, eating "fish they have cured in the summer and game which they frequently kill, as hares and partridges, lynxes or wild cats, otters, martins or muskrats, none of which they refuse to eat, as necessity presses them."

Haldimand's party was quickly exhausted by terrain and distance, however, and had to be taken off after three days. Holland finished the survey in 1765, naming 191 features after friends and prominent Englishmen. Haldimand meanwhile was completing a survey of the Magdalens and writing a description of the sea-cow (walrus) "fishery" then being conducted there under a Captain Gridley, to whom the islands had been leased in recognition of distinguished service at Louisbourg. The Magdalen survey would be Haldimand's last job; that December, while taking soundings off Cape Breton, he slipped through the ice and drowned.

North, in the Strait of Belle Isle, Cook's impeccable charts had an immediate application. Thomas Graves, the governor of the island of Newfoundland, badly needed accurate surveys so that his patrol vessels could enforce the terms of the Treaty of Paris and prevent rivalry between French and English fishermen. Accordingly, Cook went to work first on "the French Shore," charting the tip of the Great Northern Peninsula and the Gulf coast as far south as Point Ferolle. Although the British government

SAVAGE HARBOUR, PRINCE EDWARD ISLAND

JAQUET RIVER, NEW BRUNSWICK

officially maintained an anti-settlement policy in Newfoundland, wherever Cook went he found inhabitants. His maps are dotted with symbols indicating drying beaches and flakes covered with splayed fish. He had no trouble hiring local pilots familiar with the inlets and shoals of the coast, and from them he learned the local names for landmarks. His chart of the stretch from Griquet to Ferolle carried 115 place-names "as they are known to the English and French fishermen."

Their knowledge extended inland. When he anchored in the Bay of Islands and took a five-day side trip up the Humber River to Deer Lake, he had no difficulty in finding residents who told him precisely how long the lake was. Many of these were men who had found their way to Newfoundland more by chance than by intention, and who had either deserted their ships or been abandoned. They lived frugally and tenuously in remote corners of the island, but their time there was limited. Sir Hugh Palliser, who succeeded Graves as governor in 1764, rigorously enforced the anti-settlement policy and deported them by the hundreds over the next few years. In 1767 he proudly reported that twice as many English and Irish seamen had been deported that autumn as in the previous sixty years.

What Cook and the other patient British surveyors were accomplishing in the Gulf was very much the same task that Cartier had performed for the French 230 years before. They were not discovering, but rather taking stock – consolidating, assessing, observing, speculating, reporting, *assimilating*. Cook's meticulous charts remained in use for over a century after his death; and although they were little needed by the men who lived there and who knew the passages and brooding bays of Newfoundland and southern Labrador, they were essential for newcomers, and they performed well the map's prime function – showing strangers how to see the land.

After the conquest, strangers came in earnest into the Gulf. Discharged soldiers came to take up the parcels of land that their government had given them. English and American businessmen came, having long eyed enviously French prosperity in the Gulf. Most important, settlers came. Even before the war was over, New Englanders were seizing the old Acadian settlements at Chignecto and spreading across the isthmus to attractive lands around Tatamagouche and Pictou. Following its surveying by Holland, and in the wake of glowing accounts about its potential, Prince Edward Island was divided into parcels of 20,000 acres. In effect, this was an experiment by the government in colonizing without spending its own money, an absentee-landlord arrangement not unlike the French seigneurial system. At first it was not notably successful. In 1768 there were only 271 settlers on Prince Edward Island, 203 of whom were French. The English contingent included the garrison at Fort Amherst, badly supplied and very cold and unhappy. In 1770 the chief of the Glenaladale Macdonalds led his clan to the head of the Hillsborough River, the vanguard of a very large influx of Scots into the Gulf region.

Cape Breton was neglected by government colonizers until 1784, although the British presence had been maintained for a time by a garrison at Louisbourg with the usual motley of camp-followers and rum-sellers. When the damp fortress was blown up in 1760 and the troops shipped elsewhere, Cape Breton was left more or less empty, except for tenacious French settlements at the Strait of Canso and at Cheticamp.

Elsewhere around the Gulf, fishing and trade proceeded, and although the British had arrived, all of their business was apart from fundamental matters of everyday French life. If anything, the conquest served to strengthen the French sense of community in isolated places, drawing people closer against encroaching uncertainty. So, although British North America had come into being, the people of New France remained within it, and kept their ways and their language. Around the Gulf – at Cheticamp, Antigonish, Shediac, Richibucto, Miramichi, Restigouche, Chaleur, Gaspé, and on the Magdalens – Acadians and Canadians met and mingled and absorbed the soldiers and sailors who, for any number of reasons, had refused repatriation to France, choosing instead the wind and freedom of the Gulf.

On the north shore especially the French remained staunchly undefeated. Although some emigrated to France after the conquest, many stayed. Several owners of fishing stations had inherited their rights and businesses from fathers and grandfathers who had come before 1685, and they had no intention of giving up because of events in far-off Louisbourg or Quebec. When Governor Palliser enforced the law and seized property in southern Labrador, the sealers and fishermen petitioned the London Board of Trade and confirmed their legal right to hold private property on the mainland. In 1774 the entire north shore of the Gulf was taken from Newfoundland's jurisdiction and placed under that of Quebec. French errors may have lost the Plains of Abraham, but French adamance and numbers would hold the north shore.

Some French settlers' claims elsewhere on the Gulf were less secure. In most cases, they were squatters. The Nova Scotia government had made no land grants to them, although large grants were made to commercial firms, notably the Jersey concern of Jacques and Charles Robin. The Robins managed to establish a large business centred at Paspébiac despite seizures of their ships and various disputes with the British government. In time the company grew to such an extent that it enjoyed a virtual monopoly, shipping to both Europe and the West Indies, while Quebec merchants endeavouring to compete fell into bankruptcy. Like the Hudson's Bay Company, the Robins and other *jersais* (Janvrius, Fruing, and Hyman), flourished on what was essentially a system of indenture, keeping their employees dependent and ignorant. Robin dealt principally in cod, although he profited too from furs, whaling, and a lucrative new sideline – salmon.

The firm was harassed by American privateers both before and during the Revolutionary War.

LOURDES DE BLANC SABLON, QUEBEC

HARRINGTON HARBOUR, QUEBEC

Schooners from the south were particularly attracted to Chaleur Bay because of its relative lack of fog and because the cod came earlier there, enabling them to be sold in the southern market up to six weeks before fish caught elsewhere. Schooner captains occasionally resorted to unscrupulous means of obtaining fish, sometimes simply stealing drying cod from the flakes of other fishermen, and sometimes bribing employees in remote bays either to turn a blind eye to theft or to sell their employer's catch at a low rate. One contemporary report complained: "Others sell great part of their master's fish on the very banks to the New England schooners for spirituous liquors; who come to fish on the same banks or rendezvous in some of the harbours along the coast, and as long as the liquor lasts, neglect the remainder of their work, often to the total loss of the whole season to their masters."

With the outbreak of the Revolutionary War in 1775, American privateers struck in numbers through the Strait of Canso and into the Gulf, seeking merchantmen and other plunder. Charlottetown was ravaged by two of them, and some officials carried off as prisoners of war. By the end of the first year of war the Americans had taken 350 prizes. By 1777, however, the British were responding, and English privateers were being commissioned "to surprise, attack, vanquish, and apprehend" American ships. Soon advertisements were calling for "gentlemen volunteers ... who wish to acquire riches and honour" to sign on privateers with names like *Arbuthnot, Revenge, The Fly,* and *Dreadnought.* All who did so were protected against "being impressed on board Men-of-war."

The major effect on the Gulf of the American Revolution, aside from raids by the *bastonnais* and some disruption of trade, was the subsequent influx of Loyalists. Major Loyalist resettlements occurred around Cornwall, Kingston, Niagara, and up the St. John Valley in New Brunswick; but the Gulf also acquired its communities of several thousand. They settled at Trenton and Wallace on the Northumberland Strait; at Carleton, New Carlisle, Port Daniel, and Douglastown on the Gaspé Peninsula; and at various locations on Prince Edward Island, doubling the previous population there. Some were attracted to Cape Breton, and full control of the Magdalen Islands went to a Loyalist – Admiral Isaac Coffin.

The Magdalens are an archipelago of curving dunes and red sandstone hills at the centre of the Gulf. Ninety kilometres long and twenty-two broad, they arc at their ends like horns pointing east. The northernmost member of the group, Ile Brion, was named by Cartier in honour of his friend, the Grand Admiral of France. A few miles east of Ile Brion lie the Bird Rocks, "like a huge petrified sandwich," a favoured nesting place of gannets, guillemots, puffins, kittiwakes, and razor-billed auks. For centuries, provisioning excursions were made there by mariners in need of easy food.

No one knows how the islands acquired their present name. It was once believed that they were named after Madeleine Fontaine, wife of François Doublet to whom the islands were granted in 1663, but it is more probable that the name was given earlier by Champlain himself.

No one knows, either, how long the islands have been settled, or how long the slaying of the vast herds of walrus that once lined their beaches went on before they were finally exterminated under British rule. Nicholas Denys did not succeed in colonizing them; and when, under the French regime, the seigneury passed to Doublet, he found Basque fishermen firmly entrenched. At least twenty were living in a comfortable house on Ile Brion. Undaunted, Doublet landed his people and set them to work building a habitation and slaughtering walrus. He himself tactfully went back to Cape Breton, and hence to France. When he returned in the spring of 1664, he discovered that his men had abandoned the islands, leaving the buildings in ruins.

It is not hard to imagine why. The Magdalens are never windless. Hauntingly beautiful in summer with their low cliffs and long dunes and beaches, in winter they are bleak indeed, surrounded by wrinkling pack ice and swept by gales. Imagine Doublet's hapless colonists, having spent a worrisome autumn taunted and harassed by Basque competitors, crouched in inadequate shelters, subsisting on poor grains and maggoty meat, yearning for a spring escape to Cape Breton, to Miscou, to Ile Percée, to any French community.

After the passage of another century, however, at least four Acadian families lived on the islands, employed by a Bostonian named Gridley to continue the harvesting of seal and walrus oil. Thereafter the population grew rapidly, and by the end of the Revolution there were at least seventy families on the islands. Like all Gulf settlers, they were a tough and independent breed. When the islands were given to Coffin for his loyal service during the war, the inhabitants simply refused to recognize his authority. Nineteen years later, when Coffin visited the islands for the first time, they were still refusing. Frustrated, Coffin appealed to Governor Craig, urging that a cruiser be sent to clear his lands of these obnoxious intruders; but Craig replied that although he could put the entire male population into jail, he had no idea what he would do with the women and children. The shame of the Acadian deportations was still fresh in British memories. As for the islanders, they maintained that their presence was quite legal because when they had arrived the islands were the possession of Newfoundland, and that government had allowed them undisturbed possession since 1685. Besides, they said, two-thirds of the population had been born on the islands. The Magdalens were home.

Long after Coffin's death an accommodation was worked out. Nevertheless, by 1900 very few residents owned land, and the arrival of surveyors and lawyers is said to have driven many *madelinots* to less regulated corners of the Gulf, notably the north shore. Other families stayed because even with the

ABOVE: CHETICAMP, CAPE BRETON ISLAND, NOVA SCOTIA

OPPOSITE: GREENLY ISLAND, QUEBEC

new restrictions the living was good and the catch was relatively easy. One household is reported to have made $50,000 on the lobster catch in 1900, and rich shoals of cod, mackerel, and herring on the offshore banks provided most fishermen with a reliable livelihood.

The islands today are prosperous, bright, windswept, and indescribably beautiful. Nowhere else on the Gulf, except perhaps at Caraquet, is the French élan so evident – in the colour and location of the homes, in the movement of long-skirted women, in the unique and graceful stern design of the boats, and in the soaring sense of space and freedom.

Although the islands are now linked by a road that follows the old tracks taken by residents who drove between them at low tide, the road, somehow, does not impose in the way that roads do elsewhere. Perhaps the archipelago has preserved itself by its sheer insularity, for on all sides it must come to terms with the sea. The presence of troops of bicyclists, red flags swaying, keeps the road human, and the incessant wind, an immense cocoon, suggests that no matter what despoliations happen elsewhere, the Magdalens will stay impervious. Illusory perhaps – but a sense of timelessness distinguishes the islands. Sky and sea and wind are so vast; man's works so insignificant.

Two features make the Magdalens particularly attractive for campers and hikers. First, the beaches. They are long and wonderful. Not only do they embrace the islands with spindly arms from one end to the other, but at several points they enclose still lagoons. Here there are geese in abundance, and black duck, teal, merganser, plover, curlew, and stalking heron. Here it is possible to walk the shore for ten miles, to hear the wind and the rolling of the surf behind the dunes, and not to see another human soul.

Hills are the Magdalens' second delight. Soft, eroded, a delicate mixture of verdure and sea-worn red bluffs, the hills are treeless and bushless domes, criss-crossed by the paths of grazing cattle. Below in the surf are the pedestals and arches of cliffs long since crumbled into the sea – polished grotesques and sentinels. And beyond these is the Gulf, one with the sky itself. To watch a summer sunset from a Magdalen hill is to observe the majesty of the Gulf, and to know that timelessness in which the destination is the journey.

After the American Revolution and the resettlement of Loyalist refugees, the lands around the Gulf were administered by five colonial governments – Newfoundland, Nova Scotia, New Brunswick, Prince Edward Island, and Quebec – and the Gulf had acquired the jurisdictions it would retain until the present.

New Brunswick brought a thriving new commerce into the Gulf. Loyalist settlers noted the potential profits to be made from the timber trade, but for a time their ambitions were kept in check by tight Crown powers which reserved all trees for the Royal Navy. The symbol of Crown ownership

PRINCE EDWARD ISLAND NATIONAL PARK

CORMORANTS, NEAR PICTOU, NOVA SCOTIA

LES MÉCHINS, GASPÉ PENINSULA, QUEBEC

was a broad arrow stencilled into the tree, and government timber cruisers assiduously spread it throughout the northern colonies. Great Britain's loss of New England had meant the end of a ready supply of pine for masts and spars, and with Baltic sources also in jeopardy the Admiralty turned to the forests of the Gulf and the Bay of Fundy. Prince Edward Island was quickly cleared, and the cutters moved into the deep forests of the Miramichi. One after the other the great white pines fell and were shipped out across the Gulf. Hundreds of square miles were cleared and many fortunes were made from this plundering, either directly from the trade or from the symbiotic shipyards. The ugly results of the depredation remain to this day. It is almost as if, as one writer noted, the settlers and their descendants "seem cordially to hate a tree."

When the market for masts and spars was exhausted, the industry turned to the square-timber trade, a cutting technique which required that each log would ideally be "die-cut," that is, squared evenly over its entire length for convenient storing in the holds of timber ships. This wasteful process left about 36 per cent of each tree lying in chips on the forest floor, and required further trimming when the log was eventually handsawn into boards. Unfortunately, squaring timber for aesthetic reasons persisted long after the timber ships had ceased to cross the Gulf on their way to Britain.

The advent of a new war with France in 1793, the last and the longest, brought fresh prosperity to the Gulf through renewed demand for timber and other supplies. Some small movement of population had occurred during the French Revolution when Royalists from St. Pierre and Miquelon emigrated to the Magdalens, but Bonaparte's wars meant that French ships were occupied elsewhere, and English squatters moved along the "French Shore" with impunity. With the declaration of peace, the various claims on this shore were more warmly contested. Elsewhere in the Gulf, populations increased; but they did not change noticeably in composition after the 1790 influx of Highlanders to Prince Edward Island and Cape Breton, following their expulsion from their glens to make way for landlords' sheep. Their numbers were swollen further by fishermen from Skye in the early 1800s, and soon Cape Breton acquired its distinctive Gaelic character.

In 1803 an experiment in colonizing Prince Edward Island was conducted by Thomas Douglas, Lord Selkirk, with support from two old friends who shared his concern for the plight of the Highlanders – Sir Walter Scott and Robert Burns. Selkirk had acquired 80,000 acres at Point Prim, and he brought 800 settlers to this land in three ships, *Polly*, *Dykes*, and *Oughton*. During the voyage the *Polly* was intercepted by a British warship looking for men to impress into the navy, but the captain protected his passengers by the simple ruse of saying that his craft was infected with ship's fever – typhus.

The newcomers called their settlement Belfast after "La Belle Face," the abandoned French

MARSOUI, GASPÉ PENINSULA, QUEBEC

PISTOLET BAY, STRAIT OF BELLE ISLE, NEWFOUNDLAND

settlement in the same location, and the experiment ultimately proved so successful that it encouraged Selkirk to attempt a more ambitious scheme at Red River a few years later. Across the Northumberland Strait at Pictou, the Highlanders who had arrived on the ship *Hector*, in 1773, had also forged a frugal, stable, and prosperous community.

When the Treaties of Paris were signed in 1815, the south shores of the Gulf were settled by industrious inhabitants who did not rely entirely on the traditional commodities of fish and furs. They were farmers, lumbermen, miners, and shopkeepers. Soon the population would swell greatly with the advent of shiploads of newcomers from the United States and from Europe. Indians throughout the Gulf would suddenly discover, to their dismay, that their resource base had been exhausted or pre-empted by others, and that their best hope for survival lay in the narrow reserves and the cool charity of the whites. With their passage from the woods, and with the dawn of the new century, the wild character of the southern shores of the Gulf began to fade forever, and the turbulence and uncertainties of two centuries turned gradually into the relative calm of farming and fishing communities.

Some areas have never been domesticated – Gaspé's Cape Forillon, the sweeping beaches of Miscou, the lowering Cape Breton cliffs. And no matter how safe any land might be made, the sea that swept its flanks would never be tamed. Even at its most placid and benign it would hold a quiet threat, and those who ventured upon it would go always with flickers of trepidation.

Shipwrecks occurred for many reasons: because bottoms were old and rotten and burst apart under the wrenching of sea and wind; because captains were incompetent, careless, or drunk; because vessels were swept off course where low reefs and islands loomed out of the night; because despite all the desperate efforts of their crews they ran out of room and were blown down onto the leeward cliffs; because they were scuttled by enemies, or by owners eager for insurance, or by the flickering lights of wreckers signalling safety where no safety lay.

Few things are more horrible and fascinating than a wrecked ship. This is not only because people have died violently in it and around it, but also because of simple incongruity – the thing simply does not belong where it has finished up. Crafted to move, it is immobilized; fitted with love and skill, it is splintered; sent prayerfully onto the sea it has come back with a frightful reminder of the insignificance of man and his works.

Wrecks have occurred in the Gulf since the beginning of navigation, and countless small fishing boats have vanished there without a trace. Memorable storms have taken dozens at a time, and every small port has its history of loss.

The risks of travelling on the Gulf late in the year have been graphically recorded in a little

ST. LUNAIRE BAY, NEWFOUNDLAND

OVERLEAF, LEFT: THE NORTH SHORE, QUEBEC

THE BAY OF ISLANDS, NEAR CORNERBROOK, NEWFOUNDLAND

OVERLEAF, RIGHT: FOG, NEAR ST. AUGUSTIN, QUEBEC

SAND DUNES, NORTH COAST, PRINCE EDWARD ISLAND

ESCUMINAC, MIRAMICHI BAY, NEW BRUNSWICK

book called *Ensign Prenties's Narrative: A Castaway on Cape Breton.* In the midst of the American Revolution, on 17 November 1780, Prenties left Quebec aboard the brigantine *St. Lawrence.* He was bound to New York, carrying dispatches from Governor Haldimand to Sir Henry Clinton. Another young ensign was sent in a schooner at the same time, bearing identical dispatches to the same destination; clearly, Haldimand knew the perils of early-winter travel in the Gulf. The schooner was wrecked on Anticosti with the loss of all hands, and the *St. Lawrence,* after a harrowing four-day series of tacks between Anticosti and Cap des Rosiers, finally entered the body of the Gulf. So severe was the storm and so leaky was the *St. Lawrence* that the exhausted crew finally had to be bribed with pints of wine to stay at the pumps. The captain, who had lain drunk in his bunk since leaving Quebec, was finally washed up on deck by a sea which smashed through the windows of his cabin, and he arrived just in time to watch his ship pass through the Magdalen Islands. Finally, chilled and worn out, the crew abandoned the frozen pumps, resigning themselves to their fate and swilling whatever liquor remained while the ship, kept afloat only by its cargo of timber, wallowed helplessly towards Cape Breton.

She struck at the Margaree River, after narrowly avoiding the island, and was pounded high onto the beach by the surf. Some of the crew were so drunk that they had difficulty in getting ashore. Most of the survivors were frostbitten and famished. As the days passed, they turned to cannibalism, the age-old last resort. Prenties and some companions made an incredible journey in the ship's boat (which was so leaky they finally took it ashore and sheathed it with ice), up the entire Gulf coast of Cape Breton, around Cape North, and down the Atlantic side. They were found by Indian hunters on 28 February 1781, almost four and one-half months after leaving Quebec.

They had survived in the depths of winter on one of the most awesome and inhospitable coasts of the Gulf. Of this section Samuel Holland wrote, " ... exceedingly rocky and mountainous ... & often the Surveying Party was brought to a starving Condition, as they could not provide themselves with Provisions, from the Schooner Boat ... when the Wind was off Shore, & when on the Contrary it blew on, she was obliged for safety to go round Cape North for a harbour. In short there is scarce a Place, hereabouts without the Remains of Wrecks."

Prenties's tale is a typical account of the fate suffered by many ships' crews and passengers in the Gulf during the seventeenth and eighteenth centuries. It is unusual only in that it exists, since most shipwreck victims in those years either did not survive or lacked the skill and inclination to record their adventures.

By the nineteenth century the situation had changed. More and larger ships, sometimes carrying hundreds of immigrants, were crossing a Gulf which was fairly well populated. When one foundered, the disaster was well recorded by inhabitants, by survivors, and by increasingly concerned authorities.

NEAR LES MÉCHINS, GASPÉ PENINSULA, QUEBEC

Typical of the disasters that occurred in these years was one commemorated in a cairn near Cap des Rosiers: "Sacred to the memory of 187 Irish immigrants from Slico, [sic] wrecked here on April 28th, 1847. Ship *Garricks* of Whitehaven. 87 are buried here. Pray for their souls." Of the 187, only half a dozen survived. One hundred years after the disaster, the bell of the ship was found on the other side of the Gulf, and it has now been included in the little monument.

Great capes were, of course, very dangerous to sailing vessels because of the turbulence they bred and the difficulties in rounding them in a gale. The perils of Cap des Rosiers are belied by its tranquil name and by the swaying meadows on its crest; in fact, it has probably seen more shipwrecks than any other promontory in Canada.

Only the islands have taken a greater toll. One hundred and eighty-one wrecks are known to have occurred on or just off the Magdalens since the *Essex* went down off Deadman Rock in 1741, and many English families at Old Harry and Entry Island are descended from wreck survivors. Champlain's early name for the islands, "Iles Ramées," was probably given because of the slender points that curve like sharp horns towards westbound ships. On one of these, at the extreme northern end of East Island where walrus had once lined the *écoucherie* in their thousands, there occurred another of the many disasters involving Irish immigrants. This time it was a 626-ton barque, *Miracle*, that foundered 19 May 1847. She was carrying 400 people, and at least 150 of them are buried on the spot in a common grave.

Visiting such a place on a peaceful day, with a gentle surf washing across flat sand, one requires imagination to understand how such a tragedy could happen. Why could people not simply swim, or even walk, ashore? It is necessary to imagine a wild east wind, and immense rollers breaking 400 strides offshore, and the ship keeling over as she strikes, her masts toppling in a tangle of rigging and splintering wood, bursting out of their steps and smashing up like huge mauls through the decks. It is necessary to imagine the shock of the sea, and tons of green water rolling over the corpse of the ship, and people struggling amidst surging foam and flotsam. One account describes bodies frozen to the decks under four metres of ice. It is necessary, finally, to imagine the remorseless undertow sucking everything back down into the depths.

Anticosti, the other wild island to the north, must surely have surpassed the Magdalens' toll of 181 ships. At some points, Anticosti's limestone reefs protrude three kilometres into the Gulf. One writer described the island as "a stern sentinel guarding the richness and loveliness within ... hopelessly inhospitable ... perilous ... cruel ... sterile ... "

One of the first ships to come to grief there was the brigantine *Mary*, of Phips's unfortunate Quebec squadron. Only seventeen from a crew of seventy-six survived. In the decade before 1880 alone,

TADOUSSAC, QUEBEC

the number of Anticosti wrecks is estimated at 106. Even taking into account that Anticosti was a favourite spot to recoup losses by claiming insurance, this was a formidable toll.

The sheer size of the island and the fact that it was rarely visited except by Eskimos and Indians who crossed the thirty-two kilometres from Mingan for the hunting (the island's name derives from *natistcoti*, "the hunting-grounds for the bear"), meant that castaways there were unlikely to find succour. Captains tended to give Anticosti a wide berth. Consequently, stranding on the island, particularly late in the year, meant death unless the survivors were very healthy, very resourceful, and very well supplied.

One account of survival has been left by a Recollet named Emmanuel Crespel, who was wrecked on the south shore of Anticosti in 1736. Crespel's account of his journey for help to Mingan, about 240 kilometres from the wreck, reads much like Prenties's, complete with frostbite, famine, and a springtime rescue by Indians.

In 1796 a bizarre incident occurred on the same south coast of Anticosti when the *Active*, a ship of thirty-two guns carrying Lord Dorchester and his lady to England, grounded on a reef. After strenuous efforts to refloat her had failed, a mixed party of seamen and marines mutinied, left the ship taking arms and provisions, and fled into the woods. After one brief skirmish with troops sent to capture them they were never seen again.

Because of the profusion of wrecks on Anticosti, the government in 1810 established emergency supply posts at Fox Bay and Ellis Bay, and at the mouth of the Jupiter River. Signposts gave guidance along the shore and, later, cabins were built. These shelters, however, did not save the passengers and crew of the *Granicus*, a timber ship driven by storms onto Anticosti not far from Fox Bay in 1828. Exactly what happened to the survivors will never be known, since the written records have all vanished – except for one: an affidavit sworn the following spring by one Basile Giasson, a schooner captain who took shelter early that May in Fox Bay. Inside the cabins, Giasson and his crew found the butchered, hung, cooked, and salted remains of perhaps twenty people, in various stages of putrefaction. They also found a large, well fed man, comfortably slung in his hammock: dead.

Three years after the macabre *Granicus* incident the first lighthouse was built on Anticosti, and it was followed by the swift construction of others at Heath Point, West Point, and South Point. By the middle of the nineteenth century 2,000 ships a year were passing Anticosti, and no matter how efficient the lights and the fog-guns were, they were no guarantee against human error, or against the Labrador fogs which smothered the island. The wreckings continued, and Anticosti became known as "the graveyard of the Gulf."

The nineteenth century was the great period for lighthouses. The earliest lights on the Gulf had simply been bonfires set atop the cliffs. These were followed by the earliest known masonry

lighthouse in Canada, at Louisbourg. By the end of the 1700s other towers had begun to appear on the coasts, but it was Victorian technology that made possible the wave-swept, stone and steel structures with which we are familiar. Many nineteenth-century lighthouses remain in operation throughout the Gulf: three on Anticosti; two at opposite ends of the north shore, Pointe Amour and Pointe des Monts; four on the Gaspé Peninsula; four through the Strait of Northumberland and on Cape North; nine on Prince Edward Island; three on St. Paul Island, the Bird Rocks, and the Magdalens; and three on the west coast of Newfoundland. There are also three at the northern entrance to the Gulf: on Cape Norman, Cape Bauld, and Belle Isle. In addition, several moribund structures throughout the Gulf remain as darkened reminders of more perilous times for sailors.

Every region of the Gulf has local stories about the wrecks that occurred during great storms, and about the heroism and charity of those who saved and sheltered survivors. Every region also has its stories about those who were beyond help, whose cries went unheard and whose bodies were found only later amidst the wreckage on the shore. "Our graveyard is mostly filled with drownings," said one Newfoundland woman, and her remark could have been made with equal truth almost anywhere on the Gulf coast. Headstones do not always tell the story, but sometimes they do; for example:

> This stone is erected to perpetuate the memory of Mr. William Biass, Master of the ship Sir Walter Scott of Hull, by his bereaved and afflicted widow. He was unhappily wrecked at Bradore off the coast of Labrador on the 11th of December 1845 and after having endured severe sufferings through exposure on a raft, together with 13 of his crew and one female passenger, he perished at the age of 45 years.
>
> Boast not thyself of to-morrow,
> For thou knowst not
> What a day may bring forth.

All regions also have their stories of ghosts, of strange lights passing in the night, of flaming ships, of the shrieks of the perishing, of ghostly footsteps treading the same paths forever, and of dreadful premonitory dreams.

Also common are old stories of the wreckers, desperate and remote men who intentionally lured ships to their doom with false lights and then preyed – sometimes murderously – on the wreck and its survivors. Following the time-honoured tradition of the sea, people around the Gulf have for 300 years taken what was salvageable from wrecks that were otherwise lost. To people in isolated areas,

OVERLEAF: SEACOW POND, PRINCE EDWARD ISLAND

ALISON G.

wrecks were often godsends, and it would be folly to allow the riches they held to slide back beneath the tides. This sensible attitude was caught by T. G. Roberts in "The Wrecker's Prayer":

Give us a wrack or two, Good Lard,
For winter in Tops'il Tickle bes hard,
Wid grey frost creepin' like mortal sin
And perishin' lack of bread in the bin.

A grand, rich wrack, us do humbly pray,
Busted abroad at the break o' day
An' hove clear in 'crost Tops'il Reef,
Wid victuals an' gear to beguile our grief.

The greatest loss of life in the Gulf in a single wreck occurred on Friday, 29 May 1914. In the early hours of that morning, the *Empress of Ireland,* a luxury liner outbound from Quebec, collided with the coal ship *Storstad,* and sank with 1,012 lives.

The disaster occurred on a flat calm during a night that had been perfectly clear; but as the up-bound *Storstad* approached the liner a few kilometres east of Pointe au Père, fog swirled off the north shore and engulfed both ships. Both took what their helmsmen thought were precautionary measures, for they had seen each other, but their alterations in course proved fatal, sending the *Storstad*'s prow deep into the *Empress*'s starboard flank. The liner lost steam almost instantly, and her captain could not beach her. Momentum carried the *Storstad* a kilometre into the still night, and when she halted her captain could hear the cries of the drowning "like one long, moaning sound." Till dawn his lifeboats gathered survivors. Ships 800 kilometres at sea responded to the distress calls from Pointe au Père.

For the thirty-nine-year-old captain of the *Empress of Ireland,* Henry Kendall, the loss of his ship at that point in the St. Lawrence had ominous significance. Four years earlier, on another ship bound up-river, he had arranged the arrest of escaping wife-murderer Doctor Hawley Crippen at exactly that spot. Crippen had cursed him then. "You will suffer ...," he said.

Forty-seven unidentified victims of the disaster lie in a little cemetery between Pointe au Père and Rimouski, maintained to this day by the CPR. One hundred and eighty-eight were borne in crude pine coffins up-river to Quebec aboard the revenue cutter *Lady Grey,* a "fairy-white funeral ship." Bells tolled along the river as she passed.

*D*uring the late nineteenth century, the period of heaviest migration from the British Isles, westbound immigrant ships crossed the Gulf almost constantly. Conditions aboard were appalling, especially for the poor. By the time they reached the Gulf, those in steerage had endured two months of desperate overcrowding, dismal lighting and ventilation, foul food, and the ever-present threat of ship's fever – typhus. Emigration by steerage was truly the choice of the desperate.

Migrations through the century had also hastened the spread of cholera. The first pandemic swept through India in 1817, then throughout the East and into Russia by 1823. Another reached Canada in 1832 and remained virulent for six years. Further plagues struck in 1873 and 1876. Many immigrants were stricken on board their ships, and their first sight of the Gaspé coast or of Anticosti was through dying eyes.

Typhus, however, took a bigger toll. The thousands of poor Irish debilitated by the Potato Famines of the early and mid-nineteenth century provided a perfect breeding ground, and they brought the disease with them. An observer wrote: "Each vessel became a floating charnel-house ... the track they had followed across the ocean strewn with corpses flung overboard on the way ... Out of 106,000 emigrants who during the last twelve months crossed the Atlantic for Canada and New Brunswick, 6,100 perished on the voyage, 4,100 on their arrival, 5,200 in the hospitals, and 1,900 in the towns to which they repaired. The total mortality was no less than 17 per cent."

The worst year was 1847. Canadian authorities were totally unprepared for the onslaught of diseased immigrants that descended upon them, and the lack of adequate facilities created abominable conditions at Grosse Ile, the hastily constructed quarantine station thirty-three miles below Quebec. Official statistics underestimate the enormity of the horror; unofficial medical estimates placed the Irish dead in Canada at 25,000. Fifty-five hundred of those died and were buried at Grosse Ile.

Of the 147 immigrant ships that crossed through the Gulf that summer, all had had burials at sea. One ship left 163 corpses in her wake. A first-class passenger wrote, "The reports from the hold were growing ever more alarming ... One of the women was every moment expected to breathe her last ... The mate said that her feet were swollen to double their natural size, and covered with black putrid spots. I spent a considerable part of the day watching a shark that followed in our wake with great constancy."

At times, the captains of such ships must have looked desperately at the Cape Breton headlands, or the dunes of the Magdalens, or the granite shore of Anticosti, and wondered whether it might not be better to split the foul container their craft had become, and spill its cargo out into the purifying elements of wind and sea. Perhaps some did.

Typhus, cholera, diptheria, smallpox – these plagues have run their course in the Gulf, but the most

GROS MORNE AREA, GASPÉ PENINSULA, QUEBEC

GATHERING IRISH MOSS, NORTH CAPE, PRINCE EDWARD ISLAND

recent and most insidious one has not. That is the plague which afflicts the sea itself and the land surrounding it.

To the first Basques and Bretons whose caravels were surrounded by pods of whales and schools of cod beyond their wildest dreams, the resources of the Gulf of St. Lawrence must have seemed inexhaustible. No one aboard those ships possessed a memory sufficiently long or was sufficiently learned to reflect upon the scarcities of the once-abundant Bay of Biscay, and the irony of the need for long voyages to these new fishing grounds. Later, as stocks began to thin, who then was wise enough to notice, or concerned enough to raise the alarm, or powerful enough to act? Who would have thought that, given time, nature would not magically replenish herself, or that God would not miraculously provide forever?

By the end of the 1500s the technologies of killing and seafaring had developed to the point where trans-Atlantic freight runs were enormously profitable. The killing has never stopped.

No one alive will see the Gulf as it once was. The people of the Gulf have been reduced and tamed. Fur-bearers have grown fewer, grown warier, retreated to deeper wilderness. The great forests of the southern Gulf have been cut, cut again and again, and farms and roads have uprooted the stubble and the brush. Salmon rivers have been dammed or laced with toxins evil enough to thwart all instinct. The colonies of great auks, docile as dodos and long abundant, have been marched up the last gangplanks and bludgeoned into oblivion. The clouds of Eskimo curlews have been shot away. Whales are fewer, some species gone for good, some singing futile songs of courtship. All fishes are smaller and sparser than they were before. The huge herds of walrus that once bellowed defiance from the beaches of the Magdalens, Miscou, and Prince Edward Island, are gone forever, scooped up in the headlong rush for oil and ivory. Shellfish everywhere have sensed new poisons sifting through their filters.

Huge amounts of sewage tumble into this small sea. Of the several hundred communities on the Gulf and its 200 rivers, only twenty-eight had secondary treatment plants in 1981. Many, including towns of over 20,000 inhabitants, still have no sewage treatment facilities whatsoever.

Signs in tidal estuaries around the Gulf warn that shellfish are unsafe for eating, befouled not only by sewage but by effluents from pulp mills, by chemical fertilizers, by insecticides and herbicides, by oil, by copper and zinc from mining, and by countless industrial pollutants and their insidious blendings.

The St. Lawrence River has become an open sewer of such appalling proportions that no one talks about it. So great is the vested interest of the responsible governments and communities, so vast is their recalcitrance and selfishness, so flaccid are civil servants in enforcing what laws exist, and so compromising are the political trade-offs, that year after year the Gulf of St. Lawrence serves as a septic tank for eastern Canada and the northeastern states – the industrial heartland of North America. Currents circulate, to be sure, but only a fool would argue that serious damage is not being done, or that combined effects are not taking their toll.

One species will serve to symbolize the plight of all.

Nine types of whale, including the blue, the fin, and the right, are known to browse in the plankton-rich St. Lawrence estuary. Of these, the beluga is the most at home, not only because it lives in the Gulf year-round, but because skeletons discovered far inland in the upper reaches of the old Champlain Sea indicate that it has lived there for 11,000 years.

Yet, the beluga is also an oddity in the Gulf, for it is actually a type of arctic dolphin. Pure white, four to six metres long, lacking a dorsal fin so that it can hunch up through pack ice if trapped, the beluga is far more common in Alaska, Hudson Bay, and the Mackenzie Delta than it is in the Gulf of St. Lawrence. Only the icy Labrador Current sweeping through the Strait of Belle Isle and along the north shore enables it to find the food and habitat that make life livable.

Whaling along the north shore, begun by the Basques in the 1500s and continued by others into the 1940s, substantially diminished the herds of thousands of belugas that Cartier would have seen. As many as 500 were slain in a single tide at Rivière Ouelle during the 1870s, and even after the demand for whale oil had declined the Quebec government responded to the complaints of fishermen and kept a bounty on belugas. By the 1960s the number of white whales in the Gulf had dropped to fewer than 1,200, and ten years later, to between 500 and 1,000. Now, there are probably fewer than 350.

Once their range extended from Quebec to Natashquan on the north shore, and around Gaspé to Chaleur Bay on the south. Today, their main breeding grounds stretch only from Ile aux Coudres, past the mouth of the Saguenay, to Rimouski.

Various assaults have caused this diminishment. Ten thousand ships a year now pass along the St. Lawrence estuary, and countless small boats criss-cross the river continually. Even if boaters do not intentionally harass the whales (although they often do), the fretting engines disturb feeding, breeding, and nurturing rhythms. Casual depredations by hunters probably account for the annual killing of at least twenty-five whales, 7 per cent of the surviving population.

Even more serious is the impact of contaminants. Female beluga in particular are known to favour molluscs, crustacea, and marine worms, as well as bottom-dwelling species of fish, all of which concentrate pollutants. Mercury from chloralkali plants and pulp mills comes down the Saguenay in sufficient quantities to make shellfish unfit for human consumption and to call into question the edibility of even pelagic species. An analysis of one female whale in 1979 showed a concentration of 36.9 ppm of mercury in the liver as well as 34 ppm of DDT, and 171 ppm of PCB's in the blubber. Earlier, in 1972, a calf which had been examined showed far higher concentrations. These tissue-borne contaminants will

BOAT-BUILDING SHED, ROCKY HARBOUR, NEWFOUNDLAND

GULLS NEAR BLOW-ME-DOWN, NEWFOUNDLAND

probably result in miscarriages and abnormalities; and the cumulative effects of other chemicals is incalculable.

Preferred calving areas have also been lost to the beluga. Damming of the Bermsimis River in the 1950s and the Manicouagan and Outardes in the 1960s changed water temperatures and eliminated available food on the Manicouagan Bank to such an extent that it removed between one-third and one-half of the belugas' summer habitat in the river.

In the Gulf, the beluga is an endangered species.

Conceivably, even the beluga of the far north could yield in time to hunters, to oil spills, to other poisons in other estuaries until the last of the small white whales is gone forever from the earth.

When he learned of the extermination of the passenger pigeon, Theodore Roosevelt remarked that we had done it because we were not civilized. It was an odd thing for him to say. Perhaps, in a moment of insight, this man who had done more than his share of killing saw that civilization means restraint. Perhaps he saw that if we believe anything on earth can be depleted for the aggrandizement of man then we perpetrate enormities beyond the pale of Western ethics; and then, man himself grows monstrous.

Today, roads ring most of the Gulf. Roads bear travellers effortlessly to those historic places once reached only through the wrappings of weeks and months, unfolded at last like a rich gift. Roads change the way we perceive the land. Speed flattens, makes all commonplace.

The best journeys still are made in the rhythms of the sea.

Every week through the summer, a little ship a bit larger than Cartier's *Grande Hermyne* casts off from the Rimouski docks, churns backwards into the harbour, turns, and swings out into the deepening dusk of the Gulf. Its red flanks and yellow masts are soon consumed by darkness. During the night it heads north across the river, rolling in the ever-present swells, passing near the spot where the hulk of the *Empress of Ireland* lies. Near midnight it goes by the Godbout River, where the oldest lighthouse in Canada still stands. In the early hours of the morning it crosses the place where a distraught Sir Hovenden Walker once tacked for two days, gathering survivors from the rocks. Occasionally it will pass lights on shore, and some of these will keep abreast awhile, like curious phantoms. But for the most part the shore lies under the primordial darkness of the Shield; and if the night be moonless or the fog thick, there will be no sign that it is there at all.

At dawn the engines slow, the rhythms change. Flanks of islands stretch languidly out of the mists. Browsing whales pass, blowing gentle spume into the new light. The ship has come to the mouth of the Moisie, *mis-te-shipu*, "the great river," and it will dock here, dwarfed for a time by the giant cranes and man-made iron hills of Sept Iles.

The little ship is the *Fort Mingan*. It provides the only scheduled freight and passenger service along the north shore, but the farther it proceeds on its journey, the less predictable that schedule becomes, until the only fact that the passenger knows for certain is that he is passing the shore where Canada's history began. Fate and icebergs willing, he will re-enter time when the journey is complete, but until then there is nothing but the looking and the listening.

Shipboard sounds have changed over the centuries. Instead of the groaning of oak and hemp there is the clank of metal, and instead of the slap of canvas there is the pulse of the engine, as monotonous and comforting as a mother's heart. But the kittiwakes veering across the ship's froth have not changed, nor have the majestic bergs, passing with a dread chill in the night. Nor has the sea itself changed, nor the elemental verities of shore and sky. To gaze upon and into them is to enter a time older than all voyages, older than history, older than time itself. "Watching a coast as it slips by the ship," said Conrad, "is like thinking about an enigma. There it is before you – smiling, frowning, inviting, grand, mean, insipid, or savage, and always mute with an air of whispering, Come and find out."

History is one of our defences against this land. Confronted by enormity, we are solaced by the lives led here, by the survivals. The Montagnais-Naskapi first, following the mighty rivers whose names echo the roar of surf on rock – Moisie, Watshishou, Natashquan, Washikuti, Olomane – down to the summer sea and the ancestral fish-camps at the rivermouths. Then the Basques, the French, the first who wintered over, the first who settled; fishers and traders and speculators, desperate and nameless souls who left puny but human traces on the indifferent shore. Their legacy is in the flickering lights, and in the names.

Mingan: "sea-wolf." A beach "for six leagues level enough for a coach and six to drive on," wrote James McKenzie, making a canoe tour for the North West Company in 1808, "and a harbour fit for 'seventy-fours' to ride in." François Byssot came here in 1661, seigneur of a vast tract that stretched from "L'Isle aux Oeufs as far as the Sept Isles and into the Grande Anse, towards the Esquimaux country where the Spaniards usually fish." Two rivers have borne sand to the beach, the Mingan at one end and the Romaine at the other. Both were rich in salmon, rich in the furs the Montagnais portaged from the interior, rich in the tusks of walrus bellowing on the offshore islands, and in the seals that gave the place its name. Byssot chose his habitation well, building on the old sea levels behind the beach, later quietly extending his domain into the vaguely-defined territory to the east, as far as Natashquan.

Beyond Mingan is Havre St. Pierre, the eastern terminus of the north-shore road. The *Fort Mingan*

INVERNESS AREA, CAPE BRETON ISLAND, NOVA SCOTIA

eases in, moors beside nondescript sheds. Loungers watch. From the balconies of the hospital old men stare with the reflections of the sea in their eyes. A child scavenges bottles on the beach. Motorcyclists race mindlessly, slapping the day with noise. They and all the other effects of the road may soon roll eastward, defying muskeg and rock, until they reach Blanc Sablon and all the shore villages in-between. But for a little time yet the communities beyond this point remain much as they have been for centuries.

Baie Johann Baetz is a contrast in silence after Havre St. Pierre, and when the *Fort Mingan* has slipped up against her mooring and idles her engines, there is only the wind. It was once called "Piashte," this bay, the first of the roadless communities, but it was renamed for the young Belgian who immigrated, raised foxes, married the telegraph operator, and built the manor that still graces the eastern end of the bay. Here, for the first time, one senses the diminutive abundance that characterizes summer life on the north shore – the wildflowers first, all brilliant in the clear air: cottongrass and purple saxifrage, bakeapple, Labrador tea, fireweed, arctic poppy, and roseroot. The flanks of the rocks are washed with lichens, vivid yellow and red and green, and their summits are covered with pillows of caribou moss and clubmoss. Sub-arctic flowers have only a few weeks to bloom and reproduce themselves, and their astonishing brilliance is an attempt to attract the few pollinating insects. Magically, that brilliance is enhanced by the silence, and by the furtive passages of upland birds, and by the presence of the sea-fowl scooting low across the waves, or hanging in the updrafts from offshore islands. Audubon counted 200 species here.

At each port of call from Baie Johann Baetz northward to Blanc Sablon, one glimpses a closed and careful world. There are no signs. Everything and everyone is public, and so it must be if the tough adhesive of mutual aid is to hold All share the atmosphere of quiet self-reliance, yet each is unique, its characteristics sometimes subtle, sometimes not. At Natashquan, young pilgrims disembark onto the crowded dock and carry their knapsacks and guitars around the various groups – festive families, self-protective clumps of teenage girls, knots of alert Montagnais – and up the dusty two kilometres of road towards the village, for this is the birthplace of the poet Gilles Vigneault, who sang that his country was snow and winter. At Natashquan, away from the refuse of the docks, one is surprised by the extraordinary colour of rocks like walrus hide, and by the brilliance that leaps from wild iris in the crevices, and by the windswept majesty of the bay. Sunlight folds into moulded silver along the rocks, and crystallizes into diamonds flung from the tips of the sea.

Natashquan means "where the seals land." The river sweeps down from deep in the interior, tumbling to the sea at last in a final exuberance of falls and rapids. Flanking its estuary to the east is Pointe du Vieux Poste, at the tip of Natashquan Point; and to the west a magnificent beach curves six kilometres to the village. It was here on 5 August 1534 that Cartier met the Indians who told him that

DEER, PATATE RIVER, ANTICOSTI ISLAND, QUEBEC

SERPENTINE TABLELAND, NEAR WOODY POINT, NEWFOUNDLAND

they had come from "La Grande Baie," meaning the Straits of Belle Isle, and that other ships from France had already turned for home, laden with fish. Cartier named the place Cap Thiennot, after their chief.

Past Natashquan, the *Fort Mingan* swings out and away from the coast, passing in the night the mouths of great rivers where the North West Company once traded, and the French before them: Kegaska first, and then Musquaro, where the post was so cunningly concealed that it escaped marauding American privateers in 1775, and where one of the earliest attempts at farming was made. "There are two cows at Masquaro," wrote James McKenzie in 1808, "which have lately died for want of grass, and two superannuated cats were the only domestic animals to be seen. We saw no cattle higher up the Saguenay than Chicoutimi, nor lower down the St. Lawrence than Mingan. There is something very unaccountable either in the herbs or air of this coast, which makes the cattle as wild and unruly as its other inhabitants. The Jesuits thought it was owing to the grass."

The *Fort Mingan* passes the Washikuti as well, and the Olomane, the "red earth" river, where peoples of this coast once gathered for religious rites. It passes the Etamamu, and all the isolated dwellings in between, and it does not stop again until it has swung north and entered the archipelago of Mecatina.

Mecatina means "large mountain," and the area takes its name either from Little Mecatina Island, which rises to a height of 150 metres, or from the Mecatina Heights on the mainland, at 270 metres an imposing landmark. Myriad tiny islands have long made the area a favoured haunt of seals, and by 1739 Jean-Baptiste Pommereau had established a thriving industry here, based on his schooner, *Louise*, which coasted down from Quebec each fall carrying winter sealers and their supplies, and returned in the spring, laden with pelts and oil.

Tucked into this sprawling archipelago today are four communities. Two are English, two French. Harrington Harbour probably takes its name from Charles Stanhope, the third Earl of Harrington, who served with Wolfe on the Plains of Abraham and was later aide-de-camp to John Burgoyne during the American Revolution. Like Mutton Bay, about forty-eight kilometres to the north, Harrington Harbour is staunchly English. Blunt, frill-less houses grip the rocks wherever there is purchase, polished outside by wind and inside by feminine industry. Scattered around them on the rocks the nets lie drying, weighted by killicks and grapples, floats and buoys. At Harrington there is a proper boardwalk leading up to the hospital built in 1907 by Doctor Wilfred Grenfell's Deep Sea Mission.

At Mutton Bay, the rock alone is good enough for walking on. Here and there, spidery stages stretch from it into the sea, bearing tubs and cleaning tables on their backs, attended by bobbing gulls and by white boats drifting on long painters. There is little at these villages – or at Tête-à-la-Baleine and La Tabatière, their French counterparts – that would surprise any visitor from the 1500s except, perhaps, the colours. The vivid shades beloved by the people of the Gulf have transformed the grey-black of weathered cedar, and the villages are a sprightly mixture of green, yellow, and orange, as well as the traditional British maritime colours of white and red. Wherever possible, the houses are sheltered by hills to their west, so that, viewed from their harbours, they are backed by the brown Shield slopes and by swatches of verdure in the little valleys.

But they are oriented, always, towards the sea. Each has its view of the bay, its way of watching for boats. There is in their alignments a pristine and elemental correctness.

After the ruggedness of the sea-swept shore outside, the estuary of the St. Augustin River is remarkably peaceful and sheltered. Here the shoreline is broken into a maze of islands and harbours that close off the bay entirely and leave it as placid as an inland lake. To the west, the broad St. Augustin River winds into the heartland, a major highway for Indians coming from Ungava and Hudson Bay. Southwards, two sheltered passages, the Grand Rigolet and the Petit Rigolet (now Catherine Strait), angle twenty miles to Kecarpoui Bay.

The smaller passage is very narrow, flanked by a gauntlet of bald hills that slope to the water through hues of grey and green, through fringes of lichen and moss and wind-stunted spruce, to the pink band that marks the height of tide. On their crests, for the length of the channel, stand enigmatic sentries called "American Men" – cairns and glacial boulders. It is a timeless place, haunted by the flickering shadows of Montagnais canoes, by the creaking oars of ghostly shallops, and by crisp commands from white naval longboats.

To the north of St. Augustin, the Pass Bougainville leads to Shekatika Bay, so sheltered from the open sea that its name means "there are bushes around the water here." It was this place that Cartier named after himself, deciding that it was one of the best harbours in the world. Here also, gazing up at the dour and rounded hills, he made his celebrated remark about not finding one cart-load of earth on the entire north shore. A later traveller agreed with Cartier that the coast seemed to be "the last which God made, and that He had no other view than to throw together there, the refuse of His materials, as of no use to mankind."

The *Fort Mingan* will make no stops between St. Augustin and Blanc Sablon. It will pass by Cartier's beloved Shekatika. It will also pass the site of Brest, where Cartier left his ship for reprovisioning and repair while he explored the shore by shallop. In 1534, Brest was an established community. Now it is utterly gone. It was situated in a small bay to the south of the rivermouth, protected by Ile Lizotte and Ile du Vieux Fort. Beaches stretched like arms on either side, and fresh water in abundance ran out of the hills behind. French vessels moved in and out freely, buying from local fishermen who worked under various contracts and agreements with the seigneurs of large concessions.

After the conquest, French ships were displaced by British vessels from Halifax, the Channel

ABOVE: COD DRYING, NEAR PINWARE, LABRADOR, NEWFOUNDLAND

OPPOSITE: ILE BRION, MAGDALEN ISLANDS, QUEBEC

Islands, and New England. Eventually, after much litigation, control of the north-shore fishery fell, in the early 1800s, to a few large companies such as Robin, Lymburner, Leboutillier, and the Boston firm of W H. Whitely. These monopolies did not last long under the pressures of increased settlement and commerce around the Gulf. By 1876, seventeen firms from the Gaspé alone were operating out of posts on the north shore, and the coast had acquired its special character – part French, part English, thoroughly independent.

When Canada became a nation in 1867, the shore probably had a population of no more than 500 Europeans, besides an uncertain Indian population that moved to immemorial rhythms. For those who stayed and settled here, the twentieth century came slowly. In winter, men hunted through the ice-bound days. Women surrounded themselves with brilliant colours to offset the interminable grey and white. When a snow-shoed stranger came, all would gather to receive his messages. Houses, like lives, were public; there was no need to knock. Mail went by dogsled. The first mailman to maintain a reliable service between Blanc Sablon and Harrington Harbour was Joseph Hebert, and he delivered religiously every winter until he died in 1919, aged eighty-five. That same year the first regular steamer service pushed past Natashquan to Blanc Sablon. The telegraph had been strung that far in 1901, much to the consternation of the inhabitants, who heard sorcery in its sounds and argued for its destruction. Progress was all relative on the north shore; in 1934, Thomas Letemplier's outhouse at Blanc Sablon was regarded as a foolish affectation by his neighbours.

The *Fort Mingan* docks at the port of Blanc Sablon, about two kilometres north of the village, Lourdes de Blanc Sablon. A statue of the Blessed Virgin stands high above the town on Cap aux Corbeaux, visible far out into the Strait, drawing the white fleet safely home at night to Longue Pointe. Fish are cleaned and stored in the timeless manner – on stages perched on rocky points – but when the job is finished the fishermen here, unlike others on the north shore, go home by truck rather than on foot. A road runs through the town, linking Vieux Fort to the south with Red Bay to the north. Spare wheels bounce in the boxes of these trucks, because granite knives slash tires often. Nevertheless, it is a road, and it has changed the face of the communities through which it passes, turning them away from the sea, beginning to nourish motels and restaurants and filling stations.

Nowhere is the tension between old ways and the new more evident than in communities along the Strait – Bradore, Blanc Sablon, West St. Modest, and Red Bay. Here one can stand in the broad meadows sloping to the sea, surrounded by porous bones and staring into the eyeless sockets of gigantic skulls, seeing a Basque harpooner rising out of the mists of the past and hearing, at the same time, the passing rattle of Fords and Chevrolets.

High up above the towns, however, on the edge of the Shield where one can look westward over endless lakes and tundra and eastward over the Strait to Newfoundland, the road diminishes and vanishes. There the trappings of progress vanish behind cool mists, and all sounds become the ageless rush of water to the sea. There it is possible to see the great bays as they were when the last of the ice-sheet drained away, 10,000 years ago.

Blanc Sablon is the terminus of the *Fort Mingan's* weekly journey, but it can never be the end of the voyage for any thoughtful traveller on this coast. A journey which is accompanied by the monotonous turning of engines is only the beginning of an endless voyage into the imagination and the past. It is the past of the men and women who have lived here, and the past of the wind and sea sounds that spoke to them as they worked. It is as real as the whalebones in the meadows, or the stone awl found at the side of a path. It is as real as a slim white boat turning towards the day's work at sea.

Each stormless morning around the Gulf, such boats slip out through the mists of their harbours. They leave from Havre Aubert, from Blanc Sablon and Harrington, from the fiord of Bonne Bay and the mouth of the Humber, from Caraquet and Percé and Matane, from Pictou and Summerside. Usually a man stands in the bow. He faces forward, faces the sea. His stance is resigned, not subdued. Sometimes during the day he is still; sometimes he moves. Sometimes he bends to take a buoy that marks his lobster pot; sometimes he is erect and balanced, eel-spear raised for the downward plunge. Sometimes he simply stares at his surroundings.

He is always small, a mere human speck, but he is never diminished. It is his figure that maintains the human scale. He is unaffected by the passing of ships and of centuries. He is unaffected by the wash of politics. He is totally intent, at home. Sometimes he is with a partner. Sometimes his boat joins others in a stately dance of drawing in the nets. Sometimes it labours under a weight of fish; sometimes it comes home empty. His stance does not change. Even in winter, passing among the floes, he will remain the same. In spring, taking the seals, he will remain the same.

He was here before Cartier. He will be here in the Gulf as long as creatures can be drawn up from the sea. He is as close to elemental as a man may be and remain a man, and not thicken into a boulder or roll, dispersing, into the crest of a wave.

ABOVE: THE NORTH SHORE (FROM ABOARD THE *FORT MINGAN*) QUEBEC

OPPOSITE: JOHN DOBBIN, INSHORE FISHERMAN, PORT STANLEY, NEWFOUNDLAND

A NOTE ON THE PHOTOGRAPHS

The images in this book were made over a period of six years, beginning in 1977. They reflect many journeys both within the Gulf of St. Lawrence, and along the sea and river passages that lead to that immense body of water. While they parallel the text in a general geographic sense, they do not attempt direct illustration of the places mentioned in it.

Most of the photographs were made with two old, battered but beloved, Nikon F cameras; a few were made with an almost equally aged Pentax 6 by 7. Lenses ranged in focal length from 28 millimetre to 200 millimetre; and the only filters were of the UV variety which – among other things – proved useful in keeping salt water off the front elements.

The film of choice was Kodachrome 25. Ektachrome 64 was used when greater light sensitivity was required. A few images were recorded on Agfachrome and Fuji 50 film.

B.M.L.

ACKNOWLEDGEMENTS

Many people helped to make this book. We owe a special debt to those numerous residents of the Gulf who generously provided transportation, food, lodging, and practical suggestions. Our wives, Gwendolyn Drew and Judith Dennison-Broad, bore cheerfully once again the absences and stresses that prolonged commitment to such a project entails. The following friends helped repeatedly with advice on specific matters: Doug Brown, the late Dr. Charles Brian Cragg, John and Janet Foster, Lorraine Monk, Dorothy and Vernon Mould, and Brian Wheatley. The Macdonald, Stewart Foundation of Montreal provided valuable aid with travel expenses. We are grateful to Canada Council Explorations for the grant which enabled us to begin work in 1977, and to the Ontario Arts Council for subsequent assistance. We are also grateful to John McPhee for the use of his passage from *Basin and Range* on page 12, and to McGraw-Hill Ryerson Limited for permission to quote from Theodore Goodridge Roberts's *The Leather Bottle* on page 150.

VIEW FROM CAP D'ESPOIR, GASPÉ PENINSULA, QUEBEC

NEAR ESCOUMINS, QUEBEC

OPPOSITE: STANHOPE BEACH, PRINCE EDWARD ISLAND

SELECTED BIBLIOGRAPHY

Baker, Raymond F. "A Campaign of Amateurs: The Siege of Louisbourg, 1745." *Occasional Papers in Archaeology and History #18.* Ottawa: Department of Indian and Northern Affairs, 1978.

Barkham, Selma. "The Basques: filling a gap in our history between Jacques Cartier and Champlain." *Canadian Geographical Journal,* Feb./Mar. 1978.

Beatty, Judith, & Pothier, Bernard. "The Battle of the Restigouche." *Occasional Papers in Archaeology and History #16.* Ottawa: Department of Indian Affairs and Northern Development, 1977.

Biggar, H.P., ed. *The Precursors of Jacques Cartier, 1497-1534.* Ottawa: Public Archives of Canada, 1911.

________. *The Voyages of Jacques Cartier.* Trans. H.P. Biggar. Ottawa: Public Archives of Canada, 1924.

Brown, George W., Hayne, David M., Halpenny, Frances G., et al. *Dictionary of Canadian Biography,* (esp. vols. I to IV). Toronto: University of Toronto Press, 1966-1979.

Bush, Edward F. "The Canadian Lighthouse." *Occasional Papers in Archaeology and History #9.* Ottawa: Department of Indian Affairs, 1974.

Champlain, Samuel de. *The Works of Samuel de Champlain.* Trans. H.P. Biggar. Toronto: The Champlain Society, 1922.

Denys, Nicholas. *The Description and Natural History of the Coasts of North America.* Ed. W.F. Ganong. Toronto: The Champlain Society, 1908.

Fell, Barry. *America B.C.* New York: Quadrangle, 1976.

Fortier, J., & Fitzgerald, O. *Fortress of Louisbourg.* Toronto: Oxford, 1979.

Ganong, W.F. *The History of Miscou and Shippegan.* Rev. Susan Ganong. St. John: The New Brunswick Museum, 1946.

Graham, G.S., ed. *The Walker Expedition to Quebec, 1711.* Toronto: The Champlain Society, 1953.

Ingstad, Helge. *Westward to Vinland.* Trans. E.J. Friis. New York: St. Martin's Press, 1969.

Innis, H.A. *The Cod Fisheries.* New Haven: Yale University Press, 1940.

Le Clercq, Fr. C. *New Relation of Gaspésia.* Trans. W.F. Ganong. Toronto: The Champlain Society, 1910.

Lee, David. "The French in Gaspé, 1534 to 1760." *Occasional Papers in Archaeology and History #3.* Ottawa: Department of Indian Affairs and Northern Development, 1970.

MacKay, Donald. *Anticosti: The Untamed Island.* Toronto: McGraw-Hill Ryerson, 1979.

MacLennan, Hugh. *Seven Rivers of Canada.* Toronto: Macmillan, 1961.

MacNutt, W.S. *New Brunswick: A History 1784-1867.* Toronto: Macmillan, 1963.

________. *The Atlantic Provinces.* Toronto: McClelland & Stewart, 1965.

McKenzie, James. "The King's Posts." Masson, L.R. *Les Bourgeois de la Compagnie du Nord-Ouest.* Quebec: Cote et Cie, 1889/1890.

Moogk, Peter N. *Building a House in New France.* Toronto: McClelland & Stewart, 1977.

Morison, Samuel Eliot. *The European Discovery of North America: The Northern Voyages.* New York: Oxford University Press, 1971.

Mowat, Farley. *Westviking.* Toronto: McClelland & Stewart, 1965.

Parkman, Francis. *France and England in North America.* New York: Viking Press, 1983.

Pippard, Leone. *A Status Report on the Population of St. Lawrence White Whales.* Mimeographed. COSEWIC, 1983.

Prenties, W. *Ensign Prenties's Narrative.* Toronto: The Ryerson Press, 1968.

Severin, T. *The Brendan Voyage.* London: Hutchison, 1978.

Stacey, C.P. *Quebec, 1759.* Toronto: Macmillan, 1959.

Stanley, G.F. *New France: The Last Phase, 1744-1760.* Toronto: McClelland & Stewart, 1968.

Stewart, R. *Labrador.* Amsterdam: Time-Life Books, 1977.

Townsend, Charles Wendell. *Along the Labrador Coast.* Boston: Dana Estes & Co., 1907.

Trudel, Marcel. *The Beginnings of New France, 1524-1663.* Toronto: McClelland & Stewart, 1973.

Tuck, James A. *Newfoundland and Labrador Prehistory.* Ottawa: National Museum of Man, 1976.